The Life Plan

The Life Plan

700 simple ways to change
your life for the better

Robert Ashton

Harlow, England • London • New York • Boston • San Francisco • Toronto
Sydney • Tokyo • Singapore • Hong Kong • Seoul • Taipei • New Delhi
Cape Town • Madrid • Mexico City • Amsterdam • Munich • Paris • Milan

Pearson Education Limited

Edinburgh Gate
Harlow CM20 2JE
Tel: +44 (0)1279 623623
Fax: +44 (0)1279 431059
Website: www.pearsoned.co.uk

First published in Great Britain in 2007

ISBN-13: 978-0-273-71021-9
ISBN-10: 0-273-71021-4

British Library Cataloguing-in-Publication Data
A catalogue record for this book is available from the British Library

Library of Congress Cataloging-in-Publication Data
A catalog record for this book is available from the Library of Congress

10 9 8 7 6 5 4 3 2
10 09 08 07 06

Typeset by 3
Printed and bound in the UK by Clays Ltd, Bungay, Suffolk

Cartoon illustrations by Kate Taylor

The publisher's policy is to use paper manufactured from sustainable forests.

Contents

Introduction

Congratulations! By opening this book you have taken an important step towards changing your life for the better. That's not to say I'm suggesting the life you're leading now is lacking, it's just that I know that every one of us has the potential to be happier and more fulfilled.

We all have things we'd like to change. Things we don't feel are quite under our control or within our reach. Perhaps you've already tried to change some things and it didn't quite work. Don't worry, what really matters is that you're prepared to keep trying until you succeed.

There is no correct definition of success. Success is whatever you decide to make it. Success is a personal thing and what makes one person feel successful will make another person feel they're failing. Much of it is about how you feel. If you're succeeding and can recognise that fact, you will feel happy and content. Lasting success usually results from the cumulative effect of lots of small steps. It's not about making a big push for some really tough goal, more about working on a range of aspects of your life.

Your life plan needs to be tailored to your life, your aspirations and your needs. The art of making your life better is to make each of the small steps manageable. Taking many short steps can make a journey longer; giant strides however can be very tiring and there is always the risk of tripping up.

So what does *The Life Plan* give you that is different? Here are ten good reasons why I think you'll enjoy reading this book.

1. **It's simple** – This book contains hundreds of small steps you can take to make life better. Each can deliver a small positive change to your life. Add several together and you'll really see the difference.

2. **You're in charge** – The book is clearly indexed and the tips are presented in lists of ten. It's easy to navigate your own route through the book. No two people will take the same path or set the same pace. You can make the book and the plan your own.

3. **I'd do it so why not you?** – I'm not terribly brave and there's nothing in this book I haven't or wouldn't try myself. Nowhere do I advocate walking on hot coals!

4. **No dictionary needed** – This is a book that says it like it is. There are no big words or jargon. Using a dictionary is educational but it does little for your self confidence. This book uses plain English.

5.   **It's realistic** – We are all daunted by people who are better at things than we are. Human nature is to spot where we're weak and forget where we're strong. This book shows you how to improve things, but does not claim to be able to make you superhuman – sorry.

6.   **It's fun** – Personal development should not be like a trip to the dentist, something you endure to free yourself of pain. It should be more like a holiday, helping you create the opportunity to try new things. There's nothing here you won't enjoy.

7.   **It doesn't cost any more** – Changing your life is not about spending money. This book is not a shopping list for things you can't really afford. In fact it shows you how to save money instead!

8.   **It reaches the parts** . . . You'll be amazed at some of the aspects of life this book encourages you to change for the better. Remember that this game is all about making lots of small changes, not a few big ones. Big ones hurt and small ones don't.

9.   **There's a website too** – Once you buy the book, you can visit www.TheLifePlan.net and sign up for my e-newsletters. You can also use the promotional code RDR01 to get one month's free access to the subscription only content. The website enables you to swap ideas with other readers and help each other along.

10. **It's yours** – We are all unique and different and this is your personal journey through life. This book is begging you to highlight sections, insert little pieces of paper and even scribble notes in the margin. It's personal to you and for you alone. Enjoy!

So what does success look like to you?

We all see success differently. Our aspirations are influenced by our upbringing, our environment, our image of ourselves and the people we live and work alongside. Success is not just about having more money, nor is it about simply feeling happy. It's deeper than that.

The theory of success

There's been a lot of research carried out to find out what makes us feel successful. Perhaps the best-known work was carried out by Abraham Maslow. He was a New York psychologist and academic who studied human behaviour in the first half of the last century. He summarised his work in what he called a 'hierarchy of needs'. What he said was simple: without the basic needs covered, you won't have the time or inclination to worry about anything else. In order of importance, these are the things that made up his hierarchy of needs:

1. Food, water and warmth – this is all that matters when you're cold and hungry

2. Personal safety – if you feel threatened, little else matters

3. Once fed and safe you begin to want to be with other people

4. With other people, you want to feel needed and respected

5. Once respected, you want to realise dreams and ambitions

In our modern society, the chances are you are already at steps four or five on that list. Success then is really about feeling that you belong, that you are getting noticed, and that what you are doing is good for both you and the people around you. It sounds simple, but of course the complexities of life make it quite difficult.

10 types of success

Here are ten types of success that are very different, but all important in their own way:

1. **Material success** – money, cars, holidays, jewellery

2. **Emotional success** – relationships, self esteem, contentment

3. **Intellectual success** – learning, understanding, challenging

4. **Spiritual success** – sense of purpose, belonging, reason

5. **Physical success** – health, fitness, vitality, appearance

6. **Commercial success** – enterprise growth, profit, reputation

7. **Evangelical success** – influencing others, promoting your ideals

8. **Environmental success** – home, garden, saving the planet

9. **Time success** – longevity, time management

10. **Collective success** – the product of effective teamwork

Deciding what success looks like to you

Success looks different for every single one of us. There are no convenient common goals, although as you've seen, there are building blocks available, so you need not start from scratch. Here are ten headings you can use to define what success will look like for you.

10 ways to define your own personal success

1. **Money** – It's where most people start, but in reality, as long as you have enough money, more won't make you any happier.

2. **Love** – Arguably the most important aspect of success. You might love a partner, your children, pets or even the view from your bedroom window. Without love, life can seem pretty empty.

3. **Health** – Freedom from pain or life-shortening illness is important. If you have poor health, you might define success differently. Many people in the final stages of terminal illness set and achieve goals.

4. **Comfort** – The human body works best when it's warm, fed and rested. Creating a comfortable home where you feel safe is vital.

5. **Learning** – School and university teach you how to learn but you should never stop when you leave. Learning is a great way to excite your imagination, stimulate enthusiasm and develop new interests.

6. **Fun** – Too many were brought up to see life as a duty and not to be enjoyed. Planning time for fun is as important as anything else.

7. **Giving** – Bizarrely the old adage that it is 'better to give than to receive' is true. Make time to help others and enjoy their success too.

8. **Medals** – Whilst few of you will in reality be awarded with medals for achievement by your head of state, being recognised for what you do is important to us all. Sometimes simply saying thank-you is enough.

9. **Change** – Nothing stays the same and nor should it. Plan to make changes in your life and measure every step of the journey. The shorter the steps, the faster you'll move.

10. **Things** – It's nice to buy things, but perhaps not wise to define your success purely by what you can afford. Some of the most meaningful purchases that will define your success could be as simple as a thank-you card from someone you've helped.

In some of the areas listed, you're probably already successful, or at least content. In fact if you're content, then you are successful. The things you want to change are those you feel are not working for you at the moment. Here you feel you could be more successful.

Working out what you want to change

Your challenge right now is to question why you want the things and experiences you do. Ask yourself: what are the things you want to change and why? You need to be sure that your aspirations are truly yours and not conveniently borrowed from elsewhere. Adopting someone else's goals and succeeding in reaching them will not necessarily make you happy. Do not be tempted to compare the size of your goals with other people's. This is one of those situations where bigger does not mean better. It only means different.

For example, you might want to drive a sports car, or learn to drive a bus. Both are equally admirable goals, but only if you really understand why they are so important to you. You need to work out what you really want to do.

10 questions to ask yourself

1. What are the three things I most want to achieve?

2. Why are they so important to me?

3. Which do I want to deal with first and why?

4. When is it realistic for me to have achieved each of them?

5. Where must I start and what are the first, small steps I must take?

6. How can I measure my progress and keep on track?

7. Who else do I need to involve?

8. What can they gain by helping me?

9. How will I know I have achieved them and how will I celebrate?

10. Once I've got there, what might I then want to do next?

Your answers will help you understand quite clearly the direction in which you want to head. For one thing, you are introducing your own values because what is important to you may not be as vital to someone else in your situation. You will also be starting to identify the people around you whose support will make the whole process much easier.

Why we all want different things

Each of us has our own outlook on life. That is what shapes our individual definitions of success and makes us all want different things. From time to time we question our own values, ambitions and prejudices. This is often prompted by exposure to somebody else's.

Advertising plays on this trait. If two beautiful people are enjoying life and portrayed on the TV using product X, then you naturally assume that you will feel beautiful if you buy product X too. It's how cars, coffee, cosmetics and even carpets are marketed.

10 ways to recognise why we all see things differently

1. **Parents** – Like it or not, our parents' outlook on life shapes our own. You might share their values and aspirations or rebel against them. Reflect on your parents' attitudes and how they may have shaped your own.

2. **Place** – Where you are in the world will have a vast influence on the way you see things. Imagine being raised in New York or the Nile delta. Has your childhood environment altered your vision?

3. **People** – Many high achievers went to school with other high achievers and so were encouraged to be more competitive. Who amongst your playground peers has achieved a lot? What can you learn from them?

4. **Passions** – You might love skiing or hate the cold. You might enjoy showing pedigree dogs or have been bitten by a dog and detest them. What early experiences have shaped your passions? Are you happy with this or do you want to challenge them?

5. **Posture** – If you walk tall the world looks far bigger than if you slouch along looking just ahead of your feet. How you stand affects what you see. If you're not tall, think how it feels to be able to see above the crowd. Don't let your height hold you back.

6. **Prejudice** – Your own prejudices as well as those of the people around you will shape your thinking. If you have prejudices, you need to confront and challenge them. Get yourself in front of the situation you don't like and find out the reality behind your prejudice.

7. **Politics** – Your political standpoint will provide a ready-made menu of attitudes and views you can subscribe to, or challenge. Sometimes it's best to remain independent and make up your own mind. Look at some party manifestoes and compare them.

8. **Perception** – The way you see things may differ from how others view the same situation. You need to be understanding when perceptions vary and not try to impose your own view.

9. **Philosophy** – A word that embraces more than just religion. Your personal beliefs about life, death and spirituality shape your outlook. There's no right or wrong philosophy. See how other people's philosophies change the way they view the world.

10 **Proximity** – Overcrowding makes a huge difference to our view of the world. You'll value other people more if there are less of them around you. Try spending time alone and then in a crowded place. You're still you, but you'll feel different in each situation. Ask yourself why?

Your cultural background also has a bearing on your outlook on life. This might create a conflict in your mind as you decide the balance between your heritage and your heart. Remember that you cannot turn your back on your past – it makes you who you are. Neither can you alienate those who raised and love you. This can be a challenge if they were raised in a different part of the world to where they are raising you. Try to notice how cultural perspectives and traditions differ from place to place. If your older relatives see the world differently to you, try to understand why. Developing an appreciation of their viewpoint may help you shape your own.

How our ambitions change over time

For many of us, we start adult life with great ambition, but time and toil take their toll. We become worn down by everyday life and forget those ideals we perhaps nurtured as students. Revisiting those ideals can be a good starting point, although it's quite normal for life's experiences to introduce you to new goals as you grow older. However, reviewing your early aspirations is a great place to start!

Try making a list of the things you wanted to change about the world at age 18. Now highlight those you still feel are worthwhile. Ask yourself why some are no longer important to you. Is it because you've learned more about them, or simply that your focus has changed?

You will also be able to add to the list those things that concern you now, that did not bother you at 18. Think about these points too. If possible, discuss this with someone you trust who can question you. This will help you to understand.

It's important that you appreciate how you change over time. This is because just as you have changed your views and priorities so far, they will inevitably continue to change as you grow older.

Writing down your plan

It's now time for you to start writing down your life plan. You'll probably want to write this on your own, but sharing it with someone close to you can also be a good idea. You might want to write it down on paper or simply create a document on your PC that you can edit. How you do it is not important. All that matters is that you do it!

Ideally you will list your goals in some kind of priority. Some will be long-term ambitions, for example to own your home. Others might be more immediate, such as increasing your income. As you can see, the two examples are linked and that's no coincidence. You will often find that by sorting out the short-term goals, you contribute towards achieving the bigger challenges.

Making it achievable

Don't get too hung up about writing a detailed plan. Even jotting down some immediate goals and sticking them to the fridge door is better than not writing anything down at all. What's important is making a start!

Remember that Rome wasn't built in a day and the same is true of your future. Don't make the mistake of trying to do everything at once. Here are ten tips to help you make it achievable.

10 ways to make it achievable

1. **Short steps** – You don't climb a ladder in one step and self improvement is just the same. Break every change you want to make into short steps and take them one at a time.

2. **Write it down** – The act of committing your plans to paper makes them firmer in your mind.

3. **Have heroes** – Study the lives of people who have succeeded at what you want to do. Understand how they did it and recognise that they often struggled for years before achieving fame and fortune.

4. **Pace yourself** – You need to aim high, but make sure you leave enough time for the journey. Most people give up because they're trying to run too fast. You need endurance, not speed!

5. **Be realistic** – You might fantasise about visiting the moon, but getting to the Grand Canyon is easier. Then again, you might actually have the skills, youth and energy to train as an astronaut!

6. **Get a mentor** – Family, friend or someone at work. Find someone willing to listen and offer encouragement and support.

7. **Mark milestones** – Mark each milestone along the way with a small reward. It's important to recognise and celebrate each significant achievement.

8. **Look over your shoulder** – It's all too easy to focus on where you're heading, but equally important not to forget just how far you've come already. Pause occasionally and reflect on what you've done so far.

9. **Benchmark** – This is a big word, but it sounds good when you use it. All it means is find someone heading in the same direction and measure your progress against theirs.

10. **Think positive** – Keep telling yourself it's possible and it will be. Let doubts grow in your mind and it'll all seem too much.

Dealing with doubt

If you start anything new, you inevitably become self conscious as you're doing it. Others may not notice anything out of the ordinary, but you might feel particularly vulnerable and exposed. It's like having a new hairstyle and going to work for the first time. It feels as if everyone is looking at you.

As you make your life plan journey, there will probably be times when you wish you'd not started out at all. Doubt can really hamper any venture, particularly one as personal as this.

To help you counter self doubt, here are some practical ways to deal with it.

10 things to do when you begin to have doubts

1. **Look back** – Pause and see where you've just moved from. Did you like it there? Reassure yourself that doubt is better than retreat!

2. **Ask a friend** – Have someone whose feedback you can trust to be open and honest. Ask them when you have a doubt and see how much is real and how much imagination.

3. **Make two lists** – Jot down the pros and cons of what you're doing. One column can expand on your doubt, the other the gain you're looking for. Use this exercise to compare the opportunity with the doubt.

4. **Push ahead even harder** – Imagine the worst has happened. Carry on regardless, but with even more vigour.

5. **Check those heroes** – Did those whose success you admire face doubts at times? Of course they did. Research their story and see how they countered doubt.

6. **Doubt can be good** – Acknowledge doubt for what it is. It shows you've abandoned your comfort zone. Use doubt as a measure of success, not a warning of impending disaster.

7. **Take a reality check** – Doubts are how we feel our way forward. They help us make those tiny adjustments

along the way that keep us on track. If you encounter doubt, then maybe you're at a fork in the track.

8. **Dig in** – If you're in a competitive situation, your rival might also be having doubts. Dig in and push on. Let the other person falter and fall back.

9. **Take shorter steps** – Doubt can be a sign of overambition. Not in terms of the eventual goal, but the length of the steps you are taking. Change takes time so be willing to slow down if it's feeling tough.

10. **Keep a picture** – Some of the most successful people had a picture that captured their vision and long-term dream. If you can have a picture, perhaps as a screen background or on your table at home, it will help you through those spells of doubt.

We all have to start somewhere

One thing you have to remember is that when it comes to opportunities and success, we all pretty much start from the same place. Many people from all walks of life who are currently 'household names' started out with a vision and a plan. They are no different to you. They have hopes and fears. They wear holes in their socks and need to shop for the weekend.

Happiness

One way most of us measure success is by the degree of happiness that success gives us. For example, if you want to learn to swim, then being able to swim will probably make you happy. You will have anticipated the joy of adding to your holiday enjoyment by running down the white sandy beach and swimming out into the crystal clear waters of a deserted cove. When the day comes and you can actually bring this dream to life, you will inevitably feel happy.

There is a spin side to happiness. That is the fact that we very quickly become accustomed to whatever is new in our life and, within a few months, take it for granted. So taking our example of learning to swim, once you've had a couple of holidays and fallen into the routine of going to the pool once a week, what started as a dream becomes a chore.

Each small step you take towards your goals will make you happy. But don't expect that happiness to last forever. That's why making lots of small changes rather than a few large ones can be more pleasurable as well as easier to do.

Working on your happiness is a great way to set the scene for success. If your mood is good, making those small but essential changes will seem possible. If you're unhappy and glum, motivating yourself will be more difficult. Here are 10 ways to help develop your happiness.

10 things that make everyone happy

1. **Wake refreshed** – Ironically, to be happy when you're awake, you need to make sure you spend enough time in bed. Make sure you get enough sleep.

2. **Find love** – Few people would enjoy years alone on a desert island, in fact most would keep themselves busy by trying to escape. Having someone who loves you can boost your happiness.

3. **Keep fit** – The human body, especially the brain, functions best when you are physically fit. You don't need to join a gym though, just stay active and exercise in whatever way appeals to you most.

4. **Have goals** – Setting even the most basic targets will enable you to focus on achieving them. Have lots of small goals and celebrate reaching each one.

5. **Build a nest** – Have you seen how pets build a nest? It's where they can feel safe, warm and protected. Your retreat may be your house, your bedroom or even the loo. Have somewhere you can unwind.

6. **Pace yourself** – Sometimes it's all too easy to take on too much and soon you find yourself spinning too many plates. I'm not advocating laziness, but you do need to avoid becoming overloaded.

7. **Plan treats** – If no one treats you, you should learn to treat yourself. Make each treat a reward for some particular achievement. Big and small treats are equally important, so start today!

8. **Give presents** – Making others happy is one of the best ways to be happy yourself. Be a generous friend and life will repay you with interest.

9. **Be tolerant** – Others will always try to pass their anxieties on to you. Unless you love them dearly, simply offer sympathy but try hard not to become infected with their sadness.

10. **Play** – We forget to play when we stop being children. Play, especially with your life partner, lets you forget any troubles and laugh.

Happiness and success are different. But you want your success to make you happy. This chapter has introduced you to success and suggested how you might choose to define what success means to you. It has also encouraged you to look at the factors that have influenced your life so far. These provide the context for your personal development.

Next it would be good to set some realistic priorities and work out how to find the time to make things happen.

Ways to set priorities and find the time

There's never enough time. If you wait until you think you've got the time to change your life, you'll never get started. Life is simply too demanding for us all and it's all too easy to put things off. However, rather like rolling a boulder down a hill, the hardest part is that first shove. Once you've made a start, you'll find that it gets progressively easier to build momentum.

The secret to finding time is not to be too ambitious. You don't need to set aside a day, then plan a comprehensive programme of beneficial activities to fill it. Instead you need to have a menu of priorities near and handy. Then, when a few minutes present themselves, you already have useful ways to take advantage of them.

Finding a place to stop and think

As much as you need time, you need space to think. Sometimes you can create space to think whilst occupied with something else that demands your time but not all of your attention. Here are ten places where you might find yourself able to think about your priorities.

10 good places to go and think

1. **Beach** – An afternoon on a deserted beach with the wind blowing, the waves crashing and your mind whirring are a great combination.

2. **Train** – Rather than buy a magazine to read on the train, take your notebook and pen and use the journey to plan your priorities.

3. **Conference** – If you're part of an audience listening to a boring speaker, let your mind wander to your own agenda. It's better than falling asleep or getting bored.

4. **Garden** – If you have a garden, you'll know it's a good place to think. If you haven't, why not go and sit in the park.

5. **Roof** – Somehow being high up where you can see a long way helps.

6. **Bath** – A long soak in the bath, free of distraction, is both relaxing and thought-inducing.

7. **Coffee shop** – A busy coffee shop is a good place to think. Being surrounded by other people, all busy with their lives, can help you contemplate and plan your own.

8. **Ironing board** – Occupying yourself with familiar, routine tasks gives you the opportunity to think. You're

busy, yet the job in hand doesn't need your full attention.

9. **Airport** – Find yourself somewhere to sit where you can see the arrivals and departures screens. Look too at the people. Imagine why they might be travelling and guess where they're going. Think about what you might do if you went to those places. Ideas and plans will begin to emerge.

10. **Stately home** – Take a walk round one of those huge country houses that are open to the public. See how people used to display their success. Then find a quiet corner in the grounds to work on your plan.

Setting priorities

You can't change everything at once, so you need to prioritise. There are many factors that will influence you as you determine what to work on first. Clearly you can only do what you have time to do, but because you're going to take lots of short steps, rather than giant leaps, you can make progress on several aspects of your life simultaneously. There are ten things though that can hinder your progress.

10 ways to work out your priorities

1. **Age** – Although most will consider age to be a barrier, in reality you can do almost anything at any age. However, you might decide to do some things now and leave others until you are older. Work out what you want life to be like as you pass into each new decade.

2. **Kids** – If you're a parent, it's all too easy to put off what you want to do to accommodate your brood. If you feel this way, make sure you're not simply using them as an excuse to put things off. In fact, if your offspring see you making positive changes to your life, they'll be impressed and respect you even more.

3. **Debt** – Owing money can be very distracting. Restructuring debt to make it manageable and less of a worry is for many a good place to start. Remember that debt can often be a symptom and you might need to work on the causes of your debt as well as the debt itself.

4. **Work** – Your boss is making vague promises about a wonderful future. You need to decide if what he or she is offering is (a) real and (b) what you actually want. Avoid delegating your ambition to your boss and take control!

5. **Home** – The place you live is really important. Make sure you devote time and effort to making home somewhere you can feel really relaxed and comfortable.

6. **Friends** – Peer pressure can be very powerful. If it encourages you to go where you want, it is positive. If you feel under pressure to aim for things you're not totally sure about, that pressure might be too great.

7. **Travel** – Are there places you want to visit, but at the moment cannot spare the time or find the cash? Find out about them and the practicalities of making the trip. The more you know, the easier it will be to eventually do. Planning travel can be as important a priority as the travel itself.

8. **Study** – If you're an undergraduate, or even a mature student, completing your course will be uppermost in your mind. Developing some goals for when you finish might help carry you through though.

9. **Caring** – At times, many of us find ourselves caring for a vulnerable relative who is dependent on us. This can also give you time to plan, even if at times it might seem heartless.

10. **Instinct** – Finally and most importantly, you must listen to your inner voice or instinct. If something feels right, but you're not sure why, go with it because it probably is.

Practical points

Many people find that money is the overriding barrier to realising their dreams. If you're anxious about the financial aspects of your life, you might start by preparing a simply monthly budget. Use your bank statements to work out where the money goes and calculate how much you need each month to live on.

Comparing your total monthly outgoings with your income will reveal the true extent to which money is holding you back. This will help you plan objectively and put your financial situation in perspective.

You also need to work out what you *don't* want to change. Perhaps you really love your work or taking part in certain activities. Protecting the things that are important to you is as crucial as changing the things you do not enjoy.

Thinking outside the box

We all tend to base our decisions on what we can see and overlook what might be just around the corner. Furthermore, we are encouraged by society to conform and not to rock the boat. The trouble is that we often guess what is expected of us and limit our potential as a result. To really change your life, you have to begin to stretch your thinking.

10 ideas to stretch your thinking

1.   **Write your obituary** – It sounds morbid but it's not. Write a positive account of your life's successes to date. What is missing is what you still want to do.

2.   **Ask a friend** – Have someone who knows you do the same exercise. Ask them what they think is missing. Is their list the same as yours? Discuss the differences with them.

3.   **Read biographies** – Read accounts of lives you consider to be successful. Some will be household names, but look deeper for people less well known that have achieved in a field you can relate to.

4.   **Cover the wall** – Create your own graffiti wall and add to it whenever you pass by. Hanging a flip-chart pad on the wall is one way to do this.

5.   **Close your eyes** – Sit in a busy street or café and close your eyes. Listen to what's happening around you and imagine what the people you can hear look like. Then open your eyes and be surprised.

6.   **Make tomorrow today** – Describe your life in five years' time, but write it in the present tense. This makes it seem much more real.

7.   **Break chains** – Most of the things we do are in response to something that has happened before. Just

because you've always worked in an office doesn't mean you always will.

8.   **Challenge prejudice** – My father hated Ford cars and said they were poorly built. It took me years to overcome his prejudice and buy one.

9.   **Explore extremes** – Put yourself in situations you find uncomfortable. For example, if you like the theatre, go to bingo. As you wriggle in your seat, understand what the appeal is and why it's not for you.

10. **Make rules** – Just as it's not always easy to find ten points to list on these pages, setting ten as the rule makes me think harder. Subject yourself to rules that mean you spend time staring at a gap on your own 'to do' lists. Sometimes the last idea you force out turns out to be the most significant.

Where you end up may not be too far from where you started. In other words, having considered the extreme, what you settle for in terms of goals or ambitions may not be too great a step from where you are presently. This is fine because by looking wider and exploring some boundaries, you will tend to develop more robust, longer-lasting goals and ambitions.

Two heads can be better than one

Researchers have long since proved that two heads are better than one. In other words, when confronted with a challenge, a team is more likely than an individual to create the best plan to overcome it. The same is true of self development. Sharing your challenges and discussing the options with someone else will usually lead to a better plan.

However, we're talking about your life, your aspirations and your future. Whatever you do has to be *yours*. Family and friends can play a valuable role in helping you develop your vision and the route by which you will reach your goals. You do however need to tread a fine line between letting other people help you to improve your plan and accepting someone else's plan for you because it looks better. It's important to try and avoid the trap of acting out someone else's ambitions for you. Equally, you need to acknowledge that changes you make to your life will impact on the lives of those close to you.

To help you, enlist the help of someone close to you, perhaps your life partner, a parent or close friend.

10 ways to involve other people

1. **Share the vision** – If someone is going to share aspects of your new life, it's only fair to involve them in deciding the vision. Some couples work together all the way through the change process. If you have a partner, do this with them. If not, choose someone you respect and trust.

2. **Sell the benefits** – Work out what your new life will mean to those who care about you. Will they see more of you? Enjoy more time with you? Or will you simply be less stressed? Tell them what's in it for them.

3. **Make them proud** – This is particularly for your parents. Whatever they may say, they want you to achieve and will take pride in your ambition.

4. **Borrow their pencil** – Of course, you might borrow their pencil to write your plan, but why not share the writing too? Someone else's interpretation will help bring it all to life.

5. **Hear their concerns** – Family and friends often know you better than you think. Listen to their concerns and consider their views. Sometimes they may be right! Remember that sometimes reaching a compromise is better than seeking consensus.

6. **Exaggerate** – Suggest some things that are more drastic than even you would at first contemplate. See how others respond and see what they recommend you do

that's less extreme. You might end up being bolder than you would otherwise have been.

7. **Job share** – Consider evening out the work/childcare balance with your partner and both change to part-time work. It's radical, but worth a thought. For some couples, this works really well.

8. **Involve the kids** – Don't forget that if you have children, they probably know you pretty well. Discussing your plans with them can elicit useful feedback. Clearly only aim to share the stuff they'll understand and may have a view on.

9. **Keep mum** – If you still have your mother, make her the person you ask last and listen to first. You may need to translate her twentieth-century ideas into present reality, but listen to her all the same.

10. **Keep them informed** – Make sure you discuss your progress and your feelings at every step of the way. Only you know how you feel, but your partner needs to understand if they are to be supportive.

Making time

There are 24 hours in every day. For most of us, these are all pretty much accounted for, so making time to think and plan can be difficult. We've already looked at some ways you can consider your future whilst doing something else, for example the ironing or sitting on a train journey. You might want to find more time, not only to plan but actually to do some of the new things you're planning.

If you work, you've probably encountered the concept of time management. Some people take this to extremes and are ruthless in the way they organise themselves and their day. For the rest of us, there are some simple techniques that can enable you to get more done.

10 simple ways to make each day seem longer

1. **Set the alarm** – It's oh so obvious, but even ten minutes gained at the start of the day avoids that 'always in a rush' feeling.

2. **Be tidy** – Don't waste time searching for things. This applies as much to your workplace as your underwear. Become tidier, but not fastidious.

3. **Do what you do best** – It's OK to be good at some things and bad at others. Try to do what you do best and delegate the rest. You'll achieve more and feel better too.

4. **Take breaks** – Paradoxically, the more you stop, the more you get done. The one advantage a smoker has is that their habit forces them to take breaks and stand outside in the 'fresh' air for a few minutes.

5. **Don't reply straight away** – If email dominates your life, don't play email ping-pong. In other words, only reply when you need to, not simply because you want to have the final word.

6. **Contemplate** – When decisions or challenges confront you, close your eyes and contemplate them for a few moments. This helps you avoid the temptation to leap towards the first solution you think of.

7. **Prioritise** – The time manager's mantra is always to do the most important things first. Remember that it is

perfectly acceptable to sometimes make things a priority purely because you enjoy them.

8. **Avoid distraction** – You know the things that steal your attention. Say no to all but the most appealing interruptions.

9. **Fill the freezer** – If you like cooking, why not prepare double portions and freeze some for a day when you've not got time to cook but still want to eat well?

10. **Exercise** – Finding time each day to exercise, even if it's just a walk in the park at lunchtime, will help you achieve more when back at work.

Adding structure to your day, with a mix of work and relaxation, makes the day seem longer. It also helps you focus on the tasks in hand at any one point.

Not giving up

It's horribly easy to start out brimming with enthusiasm and then lose heart quite quickly. It's a natural response to the additional effort you are putting in. It will inevitably take time for you to see major changes taking place; at times, giving up will be an appealing option.

The way to reduce the risk of giving up is to set milestones. These are those often very small markers that help you see that you really are making some progress. Here are some simple ways to measure your success and make it far easier to carry on.

10 easy ways to measure your success

1. **Set progressive targets** – Don't try to run before you can walk but do set targets for each life improvement you plan to make. That way, you won't become disheartened. Recognise each milestone you pass.

2. **Compete** – Athletes are always looking to improve their 'personal best' times and always do this in competitions. Competing gives you the push you need to do better, even if it's against yourself.

3. **Ask friends** – People are surprisingly slow to realise you're changing; they forget what's passed and accept the way you are. Asking them if they've noticed any change can be revealing. Go on, try it!

4. **Keep the trousers** – If losing weight is one of your goals, make sure you keep some of your largest garments and try them on from time to time.

5. **Check the bank** – Similarly, if you're measuring your success in financial terms, the bank balance is nice to watch. However, remember that money alone has no value. It's what you spend it on that really counts.

6. **Record results** – As things change, you soon forget the previous milestones. Keep a diary or take photos.

7. **Buy that car** – Sometimes it feels important to mark achievement in a way that makes success obvious to

others. Success is not just about material things but sometimes it's good to treat yourself.

8. **Feel more love** – Notice as you become more at one with yourself, the way you can sense more of the emotions of those close to you. Feeling more love makes you feel more connected. Try to tune in to how other people feel.

9. **Get home early** – Aim to get home a little earlier each week, but without shirking at work. Get to know the kids, or walk the dog further.

10. **New hobby** – Taking up a new pastime can be evidence you now have more space in your life for new things.

So now you have explored some techniques that will help you set your priorities. You have also looked at how you can find more time in your life to consider the things you want to change. Finally, you have been encouraged to mark out the steps you plan to take, so that you can celebrate each achievement along the way.

Other people will also begin to notice the changes in you and your life. By charting your progress, you will recognise them too.

Making changes

Nothing stays the same for long. We are surrounded by change and this can be either stimulating or threatening, depending on how you see it. The best changes are those you choose to make yourself rather than those imposed upon you. Self-prompted life changes can still feel challenging or even daunting, but they can also be exciting because they take you closer to your goals.

It's often the desire to make some big changes in your life that prompts you to explore the subject. Here are some common things people often set out to change, with a tip on how to make sense of each one.

10 big things people sometimes decide to change

1. **Weight** – Some people are overweight and want to slim, others underweight and want to gain. If you're not happy with your weight, the best way to lose or gain weight is slowly.

2. **Job** – You might hate your job, or simply what it does to the rest of your life. Do you try to improve the job you have or start looking for another one? Often people find it easier to move on to a new job.

3. **Health** – Do you feel you smoke or drink too much, or exercise too little? Gradually introducing exercise can be a good first step to better health.

4. **Home** – Do you live in a depressing neighbour-hood? Do you wish you had a garden? A city centre loft? Sometimes you can do a lot to improve the home you have or the neighbourhood you live in. This can be a lot cheaper and easier than moving home.

5. **Partner** – This one is tough. We all change over time and sometimes people grow apart. Knowing when to work though the challenges and when to let the relationship come to an end is the challenge. Seeking external help can make it easier for you to make the right decision.

6. **Income** – There often is too little correlation between your salary and your worth to the organisation. Are you selling yourself well enough?

7. **Looks** – Nobody sees themselves as others do. You might be worried about the way you look and even be contemplating cosmetic surgery. Why not seek feedback from friends? You might be worrying needlessly.

8. **Style** – This is how others perceive you, not how you might feel. Are you considered kind, selfish, busy, lazy, passionate or cold? How do you want to be seen and described by others?

9. **Impact** – There comes a time in life when many decide they want to change things. You might be a student rebel or an ancient campaigner. What is it that you really want to change and why?

10. **Life!** – Some people want to change absolutely everything. This is difficult, unless perhaps you've testified in a major criminal trial and need a new identity. Work out where you want to start.

Making change easier

Self improvement is rather like climbing a ladder. You're focused on the top, but recognise that each rung needs to be firmly grasped along the way. Go too quickly and you risk slipping off. Go too slowly and you might tire or get vertigo and freeze.

In reality, it's not a straight ladder. You rarely want to change just one aspect of your life and leave everything else undisturbed. However you build your ladder, you want to make sure the rungs are equally spaced and not too far apart. Here are some small changes that are easy to make and therefore a good place to start.

10 small changes that are easy to make

1. **Colour your hair** – If today's tint no longer captures your spirit, a new colour can certainly get you noticed, especially if you're a man!

2. **Shave it off** – Easier for men, but coming out from behind the beard will take years off you and get you noticed as one who's changing.

3. **Dress for success** – No, this is not encouragement to indulge in power dressing, quite the opposite. It's more an encouragement to consider adding some new, assertive items to your wardrobe.

4. **Wash the car** – A simple but effective way to cut a new image is to rid your car of dead flies, road grime, sweet papers and takeaway wrappers.

5. **Kiss your mum** – Showing those you love that you love them is easy and always wins friends. Does your mum feel taken for granted?

6. **Don't take sugar** – It's a quick win in the calorie-counting stakes and always provokes people to ask why you've stopped.

7. **Buy flowers** – At home or at work, or in the hands of a dear friend, a small investment in fresh flowers pays a handsome return.

8. **Miss the bus** – Try walking to work instead of riding the last mile on a bus. You'll be amazed how quickly you feel the benefit and you'll notice so much more as you travel on foot.

9. **Tidy the desk** – Although a messy desk can say 'I'm really busy', it's more likely to be interpreted that you're disorganised. If you don't have a desk, what about that pin board on the kitchen wall?

10. **Keep cuttings** – When a newspaper or magazine article catches your eye, cut it out. If it applies to a friend, send it to them to show you're thinking about their needs as well as your own. Do the same with web links and online articles.

You might feel that I'm encouraging you to show off or brag about your decision to make a few changes. That's not true. What is true is that if other people know you are intent on changing a few things about your life, they're quite likely to give you a hand. People are like that.

Of course you'll get the odd ribald comment or subtle dig, but believe me, these usually result from envy. Stick to your guns and you'll find in time that your biggest critic will be asking you for tips!

Overcoming obstacles

Your change journey is unlikely to be without its obstacles. However hard you try to be organised, life throws things in your way. People say that 'every cloud has a silver lining', but when you're in the middle of a crisis, however minor, it's often hard to see the positive side.

10 ways to push over the barriers

1. **Don't give up** – Difficult things are never easy to achieve. You have to expect obstacles and be prepared to find a way around them.

2. **Admit your mistakes** – If the adversity is self inflicted, then recognise the fact, seek a solution and move on. Do not continually beat yourself up. We all make mistakes.

3. **Swim against the tide** – Don't simply go with the flow. When others are giving up and getting washed away, keep fighting your way upstream. Remember, only dead fish swim with the tide!

4. **Be prepared** – Rather as we insure our homes and cars, so too can you protect your ambitions. Always try to have a 'plan b' just in case.

5. **Forgive and forget** – Some people bear grudges for years. Don't bear those scars forever. Forgive, forget and let them heal.

6. **Take a detour** – Sometimes the barrier is simply insurmountable. Recognise when your path is blocked and look for an alternative route. If the journey is worth making, that detour will exist.

7. **Take time** – It's said that you can adapt to almost any major change or tragedy in around six months. When

your life is hit for six by something totally horrible, don't make too many hasty decisions.

8. **Look for the positive** – We are the total of our experiences. Even bad experiences carry value, even if it's simply a hard lesson you won't need to re-learn.

9. **Get it over early** – There's a lot to be said for making mistakes when you're young. You then at least have more opportunity to recover. Getting it wrong late in life can be a lot more difficult.

10. **Look around you** – The chances are someone else has hit this obstacle before. Ask around or check the internet for possible solutions.

Don't be a victim

We all know people who delight in being victims. They love to moan about their lot and seem to be naturally unlucky. What is worse, they seem to enjoy being unlucky; it sometimes appears to be their very reason for existence!

It is surprisingly difficult to avoid becoming a victim. However, there are some techniques that can help you avoid falling into that trap.

10 ways to avoid becoming a victim

1. **Plan** – You'll have less 'bad luck' if you plan properly because you'll have looked at what might happen.

2. **You won't win them all** – When you take a risk, be prepared to accept the downside if it doesn't quite go according to plan. Only people who don't take risks never lose. They never win either!

3. **Be nice yourself** – If you're nice to people, they'll be nice to you. Treat others with suspicion and they'll assume something's wrong.

4. **Use what's available** – Hindsight is wonderful but doesn't help much at the time. When you make decisions, you have to work with the information you have. It's easier to look back than to see into the future.

5. **Don't kick yourself** – Remorse about what's not worked won't change what's happened. If you get it wrong, pick yourself up, learn from the experience and move on.

6. **Believe in yourself** – If you're confident about something, it will be easier to do. If you start out with self doubt, you're more likely to stumble.

7. **Keep mum** – If you don't tell people the bad bits, most will never find out. Remember, you always know more about yourself than anyone else. Don't share what you don't have to.

8. **It's OK to be you** – What you view as your failings others might see as charm. See your idiosyncrasies as positive attributes, not handicaps.

9. **You're not alone** – Accept that everyone gets it wrong from time to time. Some of the world's most successful people are those who've suffered the biggest losses and recovered.

10. **Self fulfilling prophecies** – If you think people are against you they will be. It's almost as if they can read your mind. Actually, your body language is probably reflecting your anxieties.

There's a phenomenon that people in the mental health world call projection. It's where you 'project' onto someone or something else your anxiety or feelings about it. For example, if you think that bouncers at night clubs are all against you, you will tend to approach them cautiously. They in turn might view this as suspicious behaviour and single you out and check you over. If on the other hand you do not think that way about bouncers, you'll probably stride up to the door more confidently and be less likely to arouse their concerns. Your original concern may well have resulted from an unfortunate experience in the past. The reality is, though, that only you know that.

Pacing yourself

It's unrealistic to think you can change your life overnight. It simply doesn't happen like that. Success is all about balance. It's developing the skill to weave a way through life's challenges in a way that enables you to make progress, but not to the detriment of your day-to-day activities.

Here are some tips that might help you pace yourself, as well as find more time to think and reflect.

10 ways to keep on track

1. **Walk the dog** – Start every day with that half an hour routine that enables you to think about and, more importantly, plan the coming day.

2. **Neck and neck** – Make your change journey with a good friend and help each other along.

3. **Plant a tree** – Trees grow slowly and so do people. Plant a tree outside your window and watch it grow. Make sure both you and the tree have enough room to reach your full potential.

4. **Cook a meal** – It's important to make time for simple, pleasurable activities. Not everything you do should be a challenge.

5. **Take holidays** – Switch off completely at least twice a year. You don't need to go far away, just far enough that you can't hear the phone.

6. **Do the shopping** – If you're usually too busy to buy the groceries (perhaps someone else goes or you buy food online), visit the supermarket in person now and again. You'll find those aisles will give you an insight into how others live. Compare the contents of your trolley with some others.

7. **Go to church** – No, I'm not advocating worship in church, synagogue or a mosque; that's a matter of your

own personal choice. However, visiting religious places is a great way to understand how we traditionally made sense of the chaos that is our world. Look at how the world is portrayed there.

8. **Buy the 'Big Issue'** – Every town centre has at least two homeless people selling copies of the 'Big Issue'. Buy yourself a copy and have a conversation with the vendor. Reflect later on his or her life and compare it with your own.

9. **Visit your childhood home** – How does it differ from your memory? Usually, things are smaller than we remember them because we were smaller then. How does it compare with where you live right now?

10. **Just do it** – Having considered all the opportunities to slow down, you do also need to make progress, so sometimes you need to just do it.

Avoiding pitfalls

Change for change's sake is not a good idea. For one thing you might get a reputation for being inconsistent. Not all change is good and you want the changes you make to all lead you in the same general direction. Here's how to avoid some of the most common pitfalls.

10 pitfalls that might await you

1. **Aiming too high** – If you start something you can't finish, you'll disappoint yourself. Others might accuse you of blowing hot and cold.

2. **Rigid routines** – Long walks in the summer are OK, but will you be as enthusiastic to wrap up warm and do the same on cold dark winter evenings? Be prepared to change new routines.

3. **Not thinking through** – Deciding to befriend the office grouch might seem a good idea, but can you remain sweet in the face of their continued sourness?

4. **Upsetting the boss** – If you work in a staid environment, changing your greying locks bright orange might not please the boss. Always weigh up the risks as well as the potential before making dramatic changes.

5. **Acting too young** – Are you the oldest rocker in town? Are you doing it for the music or the effect? Don't act young for the sake of it.

6. **Overpromising** – Committing yourself in writing to things you know deep down you cannot do is folly. It undermines your reputation and people will question everything about you. Go public only when you're sure!

7. **Playing away** – If you live with a partner, don't play away without weighing up all the possible consequences. Keep your eyes open.

8. **Throwing out what you wish you'd kept** – It's oh so easy to get carried away in an orgy of clearing out and de-junking your home and your life. Don't rush the possessions purge and live to regret ditching things you really would rather have kept.

9. **Being miserly** – Don't overdo the economical living either in your efforts to reduce expenditure. Leftovers are OK for the occasional meal, but then so is fillet steak!

10. **Inertia** – Finally, the most damaging dramatic change you can make is not to change. Instead, you spend your life searching high and low for the answer to your ultimate question.

Following through

You can see from the list above that the key to your credibility is the ability to follow through. You must be able to deliver what you promise and only promise what you can deliver. It's very easy to let your enthusiasm get the better of you, make bold plans and tell the world. Then, as reality kicks in, you have to retreat gently out of the limelight. Avoid the temptation to share your plans until you've really thought of all the consequences.

Equally, it must be accepted that if no one else knows what you're trying to change in your life, it will be harder for you to stay on track. When people know, they will usually go out of their way to help you. To make sure you're going to follow through, you need to be realistic in the goals you set and make sure you allow other people the opportunity to give you the occasional nudge in the right direction.

Mentors

When someone else accepts the challenge of supporting you through a process of personal transition, they are usually called a mentor. Good mentors help you follow through on the goals you set yourself. Mentoring is becoming an increasingly common way to nurture talent and to support personal growth. Some large employers organise company mentoring schemes that match recent recruits with seasoned campaigners. This gives the new person someone they can trust with their fears, concerns and anxieties. The mentor, being more experienced, can offer positive encouragement and practical advice where it's appropriate.

However, few people in reality enter a formal mentoring relationship. Your opportunity, as you build your life plan, is to take the principle of mentoring and apply it to many of the relationships you already have. Many of the people you know and meet can help nurture your personal growth. All you need to do is to create the opportunity.

10 ways to benefit from the experience of those around you

1. **Pick good brains** – You can bypass many of the pitfalls if guided by someone who's already made the journey. Ask for tips.

2. **Widen your circle** – Friends of friends or colleagues will often be willing to share relevant experiences with you. Ask for introductions.

3. **Know what's normal** – Sometimes it's difficult to know what's normal and what shouldn't be happening. See how others are coping.

4. **A pat on the back** – Everyone likes receiving praise. If people are more aware of what you're trying to do, they'll be more likely to acknowledge your achievements.

5. **A poke with a stick** – Why not share a challenge with a friend and invite them to push you a little when you occasionally lose heart?

6. **Catch an owl** – Who is wise and respected in your chosen field? Flatter them then invite them to help you catch them up.

7. **Watch the clock** – Talk to busy people. Those with time are often less successful. Make sure you only ask for as much time as they can realistically give.

8. **Go virtual** – Buddy up with people in other countries and compare notes. Email can be a great way to discuss

hot topics you share with people you'd never meet. Search for people like you and see who you find!

9. **Have good reason** – People will usually be happy to help if they know there's a good reason. Telling others also reinforces your own resolve.

10. **Don't give up** – Some you ask to help will say no, but don't give up. Ask them to recommend someone who might say yes and then ask them to make the introduction.

This chapter has introduced you to change. Both big and small changes have been illustrated, together with ways to be realistic about your goals, set a manageable pace, and consider finding a mentor to help you along.

When change is all around us, it can be difficult to keep our own life on course. By being sensible about what you set out to do for yourself, you can keep your ambitions within sight. You also have more opportunity to take full advantage of external changes that can, by coincidence, help you along the way.

Health and fitness

There's no doubt that you can achieve more if you're feeling fit and healthy. However, that doesn't mean you need an athlete's physique and perfect health to succeed. Health and fitness are relative and success is not dependent on them. However, they can certainly help. To achieve your goals you'll want to feel comfortable with your body and the way it performs. Equally, you don't want to become distracted by your physical condition.

It could be that you will choose to make improving your health and fitness a major life plan goal. If this is the case, remember that as with any other aspect of self improvement, working on your health and fitness should be undertaken in short, safe steps. Dramatic changes to diet or exercise regimes can sometimes be positively dangerous!

10 reasons why it's smart to be healthy

1. **Live longer** – We're unaware of mortality in our youth, yet the way we live every year of our lives impacts on longevity. It's never too early to start thinking healthy and almost never too late! Put health higher on your agenda.

2. **Function better** – The human body is designed to be fit. Life really does feel more exciting when all of your systems are firing properly. Decide what aspects of your body you want to change.

3. **Run faster** – OK, so you're not training for a marathon, but we all want good mobility and no creaking joints.

4. **Sleep more soundly** – The more physical exercise you take when awake, even if it's only running up the stairs instead of using the lift, means you'll be physically tired at night and will sleep much more soundly.

5. **Look better** – From body shape to complexion to the lustre of your hair, healthy people simply look more successful. How do you look in the mirror?

6. **Work smarter** – You'll feel more in control and more alert. Smarter workers get more done and go home early. Or at least that's the theory.

7. **Feel brighter** – If you're bursting with vigour and energy, you're less likely to feel depressed. In fact, both you and the world will seem brighter.

8. **Miss the doctor** – Visiting the doctor is rarely fun. The healthier you are, the less likely you are to need medical help.

9. **Good sex** – This book is not a sex manual, but if you're fit and healthy, you're more likely to find reading one worthwhile!

10. **Avoid illness** – Healthy people are more resistant to bugs and illnesses. Once one thing pulls you down, other germs pile in behind.

Avoiding illness

With six billion people in the world, it's easy to understand how illnesses can spread like wildfire. Put a bunch of people close together in a school, factory or office and avoiding infectious illness can be quite a challenge.

Simple ways to avoid illness include encouraging those running your workplace to keep it well ventilated with plenty of fresh air. Opening the window can make a huge difference. It's also good to keep the heating turned low so that you're comfortable and not sweltering. This is also good for the environment.

Finally, if you're the workplace hero who struggles in to work even when burdened by the heaviest of colds, remember that you might be doing more harm than good. You'll get better tucked up at home in bed and your colleagues will be spared exposure to your germs!

Checking your health

There is a fine balance between being careless with your health and being a hypochondriac. The human body is surprisingly resilient, designed to survive quite harsh conditions. You just have to realise how people manage to survive for days trapped in collapsed buildings, or endure horrific injuries. Unless you really do live life on the edge, it's likely your body will serve you well for as long as you need it.

There are a number of simple things to be aware of that, if they change, might be signs that you need to get yourself checked over by the doctor.

10 simple health things you can check yourself

1. **Hop on the scales** – Weighing yourself every month (not every day!) will enable you to spot any changes before your clothes become too tight or even too loose.

2. **Look in the mirror** – If your eyes are red and baggy, you probably need more sleep. The good news is that sleep is cheaper than cosmestic surgery and better for you too.

3. **Feel for bumps** – You know where those nasty bumps can occur. Feel yourself regularly and don't be bashful about showing your doctor anything you find worrying.

4. **Check your pee** – Take a look in the toilet. If your pee is any darker than straw then the chances are you're not drinking enough water.

5. **Check the small print** – Any small print will do. If it's difficult to read, you might need glasses. Regular eye checks make good sense.

6. **Take your pulse** – Relax on the sofa, then count the beats over half a minute and multiply by two. The closer your pulse is to 70, the better.

7. **Blow up balloons** – Don't wait for a party to blow up balloons. Challenge your friends and see who amongst you has the most puff. If it's tougher than you thought, ask yourself why.

8. **Smell your own breath** – If it's not as nice as you'd like, your teeth or gums might be the problem. Consider a visit to the dentist.

9. **Spots and worse** – Forgive me for reminding you that sexually transmitted diseases are on the increase. Young or old, cautious or bold, be aware of the risks and seek help if you're worried.

10. **Say that again** – Are people talking too quietly? Have your hearing checked.

Mental health

Less obvious, but more common are mental health problems. These are often difficult to spot as they develop over time. Mental ill health is often the exaggeration of a trait or susceptibility. Clinicians are less likely these days to give a specific diagnosis that a problem is a case of this or that. They recognise that mental illnesses have a variety of components that combine to create the symptoms.

If you're worried that your doctor won't take you seriously, remember this simple fact. Around one-third of all patients seeking their doctor's advice are worried about their mental health. In other words, your doctor won't find it at all unusual if you want his or her advice on your mental health.

Maintaining your health

You don't need to work alone to stay healthy. There are lots of people able, willing and sometimes paid to help you. Most of them you already know about, but here are some tips to help you get the best from each of them.

10 people who can help you stay healthy

1. **Doctor** – If you're feeling seriously under the weather, then your doctor is the person to visit. If you're too busy to queue at your local medical centre, or even too embarrassed, consider going privately. There are lots of private medical practices providing quick, confidential and affordable advice.

2. **Alternative health practitioner** – Doctors are the people we think of first, but what about acupuncturists, herbalists and the like? Don't just go for the obvious, explore!

3. **Dentist** – The only thing that frightens people more than dental treatment is dental pain. Regular check-ups go a long way towards preventing pain. If you want to improve your self esteem, getting your teeth cleaned and polished can deliver a quick image boost.

4. **Physiotherapist** – Whilst many will be overly cautious and advise you to take life easy, it's worth the warning to get those annoying muscular aches and pains fixed. Physiotherapists are just one of a range of specialists able to keep your body moving.

5. **Optician** – An eye test doesn't hurt at all and ensures that any problems are picked up early. Remember that even if your sight is fine, there are other things to look for. If you use computers at work, your employer will usually pay for regular eye tests.

6. **Counsellor** – Talking over major personal issues with a professional can take the weight off your shoulders in a flash. You'd be surprised how much ground you can cover in a few counselling sessions.

7. **Personal trainer** – These are not just for the rich and famous. A weekly session with a trainer costs little and makes a huge difference to your fitness and your self esteem, wherever you're starting from.

8. **Delicatessen** – 'A little of what you fancy does you good'. There's a lot of truth in this famous Victorian Music Hall line. Consider a trip to your favourite deli to be as important as a visit to the doctor!

9. **Image consultant** – A new look can work wonders. People will see you differently and you'll feel more confident too.

10. **You!** – Your 'inner voice' is your biggest ally. Listen to your instincts and heed their warnings.

You cannot totally delegate responsibility for your own well-being. There are plenty of experts you can consult, but at the end of the day, you are the only person living in your body. You are with yourself 24/7, so you are best qualified to know what's really needed.

Confidence

There is more to feeling good about yourself than simply being healthy. Even if your body is in perfect condition you can still lack confidence. This is in part because we don't always see ourselves as others do. We may imagine that somehow other people are better prepared or more able than we are. This erodes our self confidence and damages our efforts to make life better for ourselves.

Working on your confidence can make many other aspects of your life plan seem more achievable. If you work to build your confidence, you will also increase your resilience and become better able to withstand life's brickbats. Here are some tips to help you do that.

10 ways to become more confident

1. **Value shyness** – Deep down, everyone is shy. It's just that some compensate for it more than others. Recognising this will boost your own confidence.

2. **Take to the stage** – Many top performers are shy people putting on a brave face. Acting or joining a choir is a great way to step into a different role where you can be more confident.

3. **Don't be too modest** – Don't hide your achievements away. Display them proudly and acknowledge what you've done in life so far.

4. **Take charge** – It's amazing. When anything happens, everyone waits for someone else to take charge. Step forward and everyone else will step back. If you act confidently, others will treat you as a confident person.

5. **Start afresh** – If there's one place you go where you're treated as a doormat, find a way to stop going there. It might mean changing jobs or moving into a new circle of friends.

6. **Keep the cat in the bag** – If you start a conversation by saying you're nervous, people will categorise you as such. Unless you tell them, most people won't know.

7. **Challenge yourself** – Dare yourself to do something bolder than you would normally. Make being bolder a habit and it will grow.

8. **Accept the odd knock** – You won't win every time. One art of success is to keep trying. Don't dwell on the failures or they'll hold you back.

9. **Small talk matters** – Starting conversations is always harder than maintaining them. Have some set questions you can use to open a dialogue and get the other person talking.

10. **Smile** – Look in the mirror. If you're anxious, you don't smile. Practise smiling because if you look happy, people will respond more positively and that will boost your self confidence.

Diet

We're always being encouraged to eat healthily and the bookshops are full of diet books. It's a fact that you will feel better if you eat well. It is also important to have a balanced diet. However, part of that balance can be those junk-food treats we all enjoy from time to time.

Obesity is also constantly highlighted in the media as a problem. Less well publicised but no less important are the health problems that can relate from being underweight. Your weight is just one of a wide range of factors that influence how you feel. Don't get too hung up about weight in isolation.

10 simple things to improve your diet

1. **Lots of water** – Our bodies are almost 70 per cent water so you need to drink plenty, especially when the weather is warm or you're feeling hot. Make carrying a bottle of water a habit and you'll find yourself drinking more.

2. **Watch the fat** – A totally fat-free diet would not be healthy, so banning fat is bad. However, some forms of fat are better for you than others. Do watch what you are eating.

3. **One lump not two** – Reducing your intake of highly refined sugar can help you control your weight. Cut down slowly and you probably won't notice the difference.

4. **Watch the alcohol** – If you drink, remember that alcohol is packed with calories and won't help you lose weight. Drinking too much can also damage your health. Think before you drink.

5. **Don't skip breakfast** – A good breakfast literally sets you up for the day. Skipping breakfast is an invitation to start snacking.

6. **Don't go short** – If you mainly graze on the hoof, or perhaps choose not to eat certain types of food, make sure you're getting everything you need from your diet.

7. **Fill up with fibre** – Many processed foods are low in fibre. If time commits you to convenience foods, try topping up with high-fibre snacks.

8. **Little and often** – Eat when you're hungry, not just because it's lunchtime. Many people prefer to eat several small meals rather than three big ones. Would this suit your lifestyle?

9. **Go raw** – Fruit, raw vegetables and nuts make great snacks. They're more satisfying than biscuits and usually cheaper too.

10. **Forget fads** – Every few months a new faddy diet comes along. Rely instead on common sense and your own instincts.

Fitness

It's very easy to get depressed about fitness. There are so many sports to try, gyms to visit and clubs to join. The reality is that as with anything else, the best way to improve your fitness is a little at a time.

10 quick ways to get yourself fitter

1. **Climb the stairs** – Start by getting out of the lift two floors early and climb the rest of the way. Within weeks you be bounding up the stairs two at a time. Stairs are great for firming your legs and bottom.

2. **Walk to work** – You'd be surprised how little extra time it takes, especially if you live in a city. Two miles should take you 30–40 minutes. It's probably quicker than the bus!

3. **Use your lunch-break** – In an hour, you've time to go for a swim, a jog or just a walk in the park. Then eat your sandwiches and start the afternoon refreshed.

4. **Sit up and look** – See how many sit-ups you can manage in the commercial breaks on TV. You can rest whilst watching the programme and then perhaps exercise again!

5. **Laugh out loud** – Laughter is good for your lungs. Don't just chuckle quietly, let yourself go and really work those lungs. Laughter has many benefits and makes you happy too.

6. **Dig the garden** – Your grandparents probably kept fit working their allotment. Growing your own food is great exercise and it's fun to eat what you produce.

7. **Scrub the bath** – Using lots of elbow grease as you do your housework raises your pulse and gives your whole body a workout. Recognise the workout value of cleaning and you'll start to enjoy those chores.

8. **Jump up and down** – Do you remember doing star jumps at school? They're surprisingly good for you. See how quickly you can do 100. Tomorrow, try to do them faster!

9. **Beat a buddy** – No, I'm not advocating violence. Competition or friendly rivalry will spur you both on to get fitter. It doesn't matter who's faster or stronger, if you both get fitter, you both win.

10. **Start now** – Stop thinking you'll do this later. Put the book down and do some exercise!

Your body is important. It houses you, transports you and enables you to do all the things you do. It also has the remarkable ability to recover when damaged by illness and to evolve to meet the demands of lifestyle changes. This means that however you find your body right now, if you want to improve aspects of your health, fitness or diet you probably can. Remember that it's kinder on your body as well as your confidence to take things gradually!

Stress

It might be that your search for improvement has been prompted by the stress of your current lifestyle. There is no escaping the fact that stress and change are almost constant companions. Stress is one of the largest causes of time off work these days. It's costly for employers and can wreak havoc on your life.

Changing your life can increase your exposure to stress, so it's important to spend some time understanding how to manage it. Finding the time and focus to create your life plan can put you under additional pressure. To make the changes you're planning happen will inevitably entail some stress. All change can be stressful, even if it's change that you yourself are driving.

Understanding a little more about stress, how to spot the signs and most importantly of all, how to reduce the levels, should form an integral part of your life plan journey.

What is stress?

Our physical response to stress is entirely natural. Our ancestors were better able to fight or flee if their heart rate quickened and their senses sharpened. The problem is that in today's world, you're more likely to be attacked by anxiety than wild animals.

Emotionally, stress can give us a vital boost when the pressure is on to perform. It can widen our perspective. However, the negative effects can include distrust, anger, frustration and ultimately depression. Stress is one dimension of our mental well-being that we all need to recognise and try to manage.

10 ways to use stress to your advantage

1. **Win the race** – When you're competing and determined to win, stress triggers the release of adrenalin which boosts your performance. Only get worked up about important races, the ones you really need to win.

2. **Work deadlines** – Providing you've agreed them, deadlines create positive stress as they approach, spurring you into action. You'll often produce better work when up against a deadline. Try setting your own!

3. **Love** – We need strong relationships and, naturally, love can sometimes be stressful. Use your stress together to work through the issues that are blocking the way.

4. **Fight/flight** – Without those inbuilt biochemical responses to danger, we would not be so well prepared to recognise and escape real perils. You don't need to use stress if you're being threatened, it happens automatically.

5. **Traffic jams** – Of course you could accept the delay and listen to some music. Use the time to do something relaxing and positive, and benefit from what otherwise would be a stressful experience.

6. **Overwork** – If your workload is stressing you and you recognise that fact, you can do something about it.

Workloads can grow almost unnoticed, but stress flags this up when it reaches a critical level. Use stress as a warning sign that you're doing too much.

7. **Be a hero** – You're walking down the road and a child runs out into the road. Your stress response gives you the strength to catch the child before it reaches the traffic.

8. **Good stress is healthy** – Researchers have shown that your body benefits from some exposure to stress. In other words, you can be too laid back for your own good. Learn to manage positive stress.

9. **Remember more** – Stressful events are easier to remember. The scene somehow burns itself into your memory. A benefit of this stress response is that you learn from mistakes faster.

10. **Revisit the goal** – If you keep pushing and not succeeding, use stress as a trigger to stop and think again. Don't let the stress wind you up; take it as a signal to review, not as a threat to your success.

Why we get stressed

Situations themselves are not stressful, they simply happen. The stress results from the way we perceive those situations. Two commuters in a traffic jam can both find themselves likely to arrive at work 30 minutes late. For one, this can be extremely frustrating and stressful. The other one however, decides that he cannot change the traffic jam and so plays a relaxing CD and enjoys an unplanned musical interlude.

Stress often occurs when we feel we are powerless to change the things that are impacting on our lives. Farmers can be stressed by poor weather, business owners by bureaucracy, and we can all be stressed by problems at home.

10 ways to minimise the risk of stress

1. **Make time** – Don't be a martyr to any cause. Make sure you set aside some time every week (or even every day) simply to be yourself and do something you enjoy.

2. **Value diversity** – Everyone is different. Values and perceptions are shaped by culture and experience. Don't feel put down if others don't agree with your outlook. Try to understand their views too.

3. **Appreciate your good points** – Don't take for granted the things that make you special. Celebrate your strengths.

4. **Accept your bad points** – In fact don't even call them bad points. Focus instead on your strong points.

5. **Work at your relationships** – Research suggests that our relationships help keep us sane. Work at your relationships with those around you.

6. **Make friends** – Our ancestors lived communally and it's in our nature to be part of a group. That's why loneliness can be so distressing. Value good friends.

7. **Kiss and make up** – Don't let disagreements fester and eat away at you. Always seek an amicable solution then move on.

8. **Evict envy** – There's always someone around who seems to have been dealt a better hand than you.

However, envy won't improve your lot so evict the negative feeling. Focus on what you've got instead.

9. **Healthy body = healthy mind** – If your body is healthy, it is more resistant to illnesses of all kinds and that includes stress.

10. **The future starts here** – You cannot turn the clock back. Dwelling on past decisions and episodes simply makes you ill. Accept the past and face the future.

Recognising stress

Not everybody responds to stress in the same way. That makes it difficult to spot when someone is experiencing too much stress. There are however many symptoms that can give you, or perhaps more importantly those around you, indications that stress is becoming a problem.

10 signs of stress and how to counter them

1. **Can't sleep** – With a problem on your mind, sleep can be difficult. One classic sign of severe stress is waking in the early hours with your brain buzzing with worry. Try to park problems at bedtime.

2. **Headaches** – It's the last thing you need, but it arrives anyway. Your head hurts, you feel sick and you feel it important to battle on. Painkillers help, but perhaps you need to take time out to think.

3. **Sweaty palms** – It's as if you're anticipating something dreadful all the time. Understand that this is normal at times, for example before you speak in public, and it will worry you less. At other times, recognise that it's a stress symptom and work out what's causing it.

4. **Bad guts** – As amazing as it may seem, your digestive system is very much a barometer for your level of stress. From stomach aches to loose bowels or wind. Your guts are quick to voice their concern. When you're stressed you often eat quickly. Try slowing down and making time for meals.

5. **Impotence** – Mainly a man thing, but worth mentioning all the same. Tension in your mind produces the opposite effect below your belt. Worrying about it can make the problem worse, but your doctor might be able to help.

6, **Itches and rashes** – Blotchy skin, even just an annoying tendency to blush all the time, are often caused by stress. If this affects you, try wearing loose clothing as this will help you feel relaxed.

7. **Chest pain** – Often it's that panic trip to the hospital that makes you realise that whilst you're not actually having a heart attack, you need to do something about your stress levels. In this instance, your body has taken control and called for help on your behalf.

8. **The grumps** – Stressed people can be very bad company. Nothing's ever right for them and they're quick to complain. Notice how people are reacting to you. Is your stress making them grumpy with you?

9. **Back and shoulder pain** – When you're stressed, you tend to hold yourself differently and tense muscles without realising it. Massage helps, but like other remedies, it treats the symptom not the cause.

10. **Sleep like a baby** – Just as stress can keep you awake, so too can it make you feel tired all the time. Sleep is how your body rests and if you need a lot of sleep, you need to recognise the warning this might be giving you.

Reducing stress

The art of managing stress is to feel you're in control. It's important not to burden yourself with too many commitments so that you feel overwhelmed by it all. It can be difficult when you're in the thick of it, so here are some obvious and some less obvious ways to achieve this.

10 simple ways to reduce your stress

1. **Be realistic** – If you set out to do too much, you'll only end up stressed. Worse still, you'll forget to celebrate what has been achieved because you'll be beating yourself up for what's still to be done.

2. **Delegate** – Getting someone else to take on the task you're worried about might make them anxious, but you'll feel much better!

3. **Get faith** – People who follow a faith often take comfort at times of crisis from their beliefs. What do you believe in?

4. **Take time off** – Paradoxically, the less time you actually work, the more you sometimes achieve. Make sure you take holidays.

5. **Get creative** – There's a way around most things. You simply need to take your brain out of gear and let it freewheel a bit. Whatever it is that's stressing you, see if you can find a way to bypass the cause.

6. **Plant flowers** – Gardening is wonderfully therapeutic. Seeds turn into plants and then produce blooms all in their own time. You simply cannot rush them.

7. **Buy toys** – You don't have to be a child to play. Adult toys include sports cars and boats, but you don't need

millions to have a few toys. How many years is it since you flew a kite?

8. **Get fit** – It's been said before but needs saying again. If you're fit and feel good, you'll be able to handle stress that much better.

9. **Share** – And this doesn't mean dumping your anxieties on those around you! However, talking about the things that stress you with someone you trust does help.

10. **Listen to music** – Music has always had the power to soothe. Make sure you make space for music in your life. If you can make music, or sing, all the better. Music creates a world into which you can escape from time to time to rest.

There are also bad ways to reduce stress. In reality, these tend to anaesthetise the pain rather than solve the problem. When the effects wear off, you often feel worse than you did before. People who are stressed often make greater use of alcohol and tobacco.

Sleep and stress

Did you know that sleep deprivation is considered a form of torture by the Geneva Convention? When you talk with mental health professionals, they tell you that sleep is the single biggest factor in a swift recovery. Too often it seems extreme tiredness is the biggest factor in the slide into depression. Getting enough sleep is considered one of the most effective remedies for stress.

We all need our sleep, but if stress is keeping you awake, here are some tips to help you beat it.

10 ways to make sure you get enough sleep

1. **Larks and owls** – It's a fact that early risers flag by mid-evening whilst the owls are still getting into their swing. If you have a different sleep pattern to the person you share a bed with, accept the difference and go to bed at different times.

2. **Drink milk** – It contains an amino acid that calms the brain. It's why our grandparents always had a hot milky drink before retiring for the night. On this one, granny really did know best!

3. **Don't work out in the evening** – Apart from the obvious bedroom athletics, raising your pulse at the gym late in the day can make sleep harder.

4. **Dim the lights** – We're conditioned to be awake when it's light. Try some 'mood lighting' in the evening – and turn off the TV too.

5. **Skip the coffee** – Three double espressos after dinner will keep you buzzing well into the small hours. Try to give them a miss.

6. **Run the bath** – Take a good long soak in a hot, candlelit bath, perhaps with some soothing music and you'll be lucky to stay awake until you get into bed!

7. **Clear the decks** – If you've things on your mind, review them before you go to bed and set some priorities for tomorrow. It'll stop you worrying.

8. **Clean sheets** – There's nothing quite like fresh, clean cotton sheets.

9. **Close the door** – It's easier to get to sleep when it's quiet. If you set your washing machine to run in the night, you also want to avoid being woken when it shakes as it spins.

10. **Open the window** – Your body needs to be snug under the covers and your head breathing nice cool air. If you're worried about security, get a locking window catch that allows you to secure the window.

Where you sleep is also important. You'll have noticed that when you're travelling, especially alone, it can be difficult to get to sleep in a strange bed. That's because we instinctively like to sleep in the same place where our subconscious knows we will be safe.

If you have a bedtime routine, try to follow it when away from home. Also, it often helps to take something with you from home that might help you sleep. There's nothing wrong with still having your teddy bear at 30 and even less wrong with sneaking it into your suitcase when you're going away!

Stress can keep you awake, but it can also warn you that you're doing too much. Stress can give you the short sharp burst of energy, strength and clear thinking you need to deal with adversity and danger. Managing your stress, in all its guises, can make life easier and enable you to keep your plan on track. Remember that we all need some stress; the skill is in recognising when stress begins to harm, rather than help you.

Your world of work

Most of us need to work to live. Whatever the changes you are planning to make, your life plan will inevitably include making a living. Few people have the luxury of financial self sufficiency. Because we feel so dependent on our jobs, we tend to love and hate them at the same time. Rather as our parents probably did when we were small, our employer provides us with much of the nurture we need. This can make it difficult to feel in control.

As you work through each aspect of your life in this book in isolation, you will notice how they fit together. You need your health to work and you need to work to make money. Other aspects of your life plan will help you decide what to do with that money.

Your work though occupies a significant part of your waking life, so it's important to explore it in some depth. Let's start with those annoying niggles which, if left untreated, can really wear you down.

10 common work niggles and how to deal with them

1. **It's unfulfilling** – This might well be what prompted you to buy this book. Have you tried for promotion or a better job?

2. **My boss takes me for granted** – It can be difficult to push yourself forward, so why not see if you can influence others and gain a reputation. Your boss will take more notice if others say what you want him or her to hear.

3. **The canteen is awful and we're out of town** – Are you the only one who doesn't like pie and chips? Gather support and lobby for something better.

4. **My boss doesn't inspire me** – Maybe your boss needs your support to achieve what is needed. Encourage him or her to delegate more to you. It'll make work more interesting and equip you for promotion.

5. **It's changed** – Organisations evolve and sometimes move away from the areas that interest you most. Or perhaps your interests have changed over the years. Work out what has changed to make work less interesting. Then you can perhaps do something about it.

6. **I hate open plan** – This is difficult to change, but sometimes moving your desk round or acquiring a few screens can give you the privacy you're missing.

7. **I'm not valued by colleagues** – Find someone you trust and share your concern. It might be something you're doing or more likely, largely in your mind. Get reassured or work on any problems.

8. **The politics here are awful** – Ask yourself why your firm is so political. What are the tensions? How can you help defuse them?

9. **We're all doomed** – Most companies have their resident merchant of doom. They're best ignored. To challenge them will wear you down.

10. **No peace and quiet** – If you're constantly being interrupted, why not develop a system of signals that let people know you need some peace and quiet. Even an upside down plastic cup on top of your screen will do, providing you've explained its significance. Use it sensibly and make sure you tell people why it's there.

Us and them

It's all too easy to get into the victim mindset and blame your employer for everything. Your boss, or perhaps their boss, has targets to meet, a budget to stick to and people to keep motivated, happy and productive. Everyone has to take some responsibility for what happens in the workplace, even you!

Sometimes though, unhealthy situations develop at work and these might need you to act as a whistleblower. These include bullying, theft and danger to life. It's wise to adopt a pragmatic approach to workplace legislation and not make battles out of what in reality are minor issues. Equally, we are all responsible for the safety and well-being of those around us and turning a blind eye to major risk is unwise.

Managing the boss

Bosses are placed in a position of authority over you but equally, cannot succeed on their own. Here are ten easy ways to make sure your boss is giving you the best possible deal.

10 positive ways to manage your boss

1. **Agree objectives and write them down** – Don't rely on people remembering what's been agreed. It's too easy to forget. Always confirm what's been agreed in writing, even if only by email.

2. **Get to know them well** – Not intimately you understand, but well enough to know their likes, dislikes, fears and hopes. If you understand what motivates them, you know how to manage them!

3. **Be upfront about your ambition** – Even if all you want is to stay just where you are, that ambition should also be plainly communicated. Your boss deserves to know what you want.

4. **Make life easy** – There's no substitute for delivering what your boss has asked for, on time and up to standard. If your boss doesn't have to chase you, they've more time to praise you.

5. **Cover their backs** – Everyone makes mistakes and bailing your boss out of a scrape can win you favours. Don't drop them in it.

6. **Feed them intelligence** – Sometimes it's hard to keep your ear to the ground when your head is in the clouds. Providing useful snippets of intelligence will keep you top of their 'rewards' list.

7. **Don't tell tales** – Whilst intelligence is good, snitching on colleagues is bad. Unless they are well out of line!

8. **Remember their birthday** – Even the harshest boss is human too. Recognise their anniversaries and they'll recognise yours.

9. **Play the game** – Sometimes, especially in a big organisation, you need to play along with situations where you don't know the big picture. Recognise when you need to accept and not challenge.

10. **Give them space** – Your challenges and goals form just part of your boss's workload. Be kind and don't dominate their lives. Give them time to think and act strategically.

Seeing it through the boss's eyes

There are two sides to every coin and bosses get frustrated too. Sometimes you need to look at yourself through your boss's eyes. Your boss is probably an employee too, or if not they will own the business. Whichever applies, they are likely to be as dependent as you are on the organisation's prosperity for their income and job satisfaction.

Whatever your organisation does, your manager will have accepted responsibility for meeting performance targets. To do this effectively, he or she will need to know when things are going awry, rather than find out later. They will also rely on you to give them objective feedback where you think it will help. It's almost always more constructive to tell your boss what you think needs to change rather than telling everyone else.

Culture

Every organisation has its own unique culture. You, as well as everyone else there, have the opportunity to influence that culture. In fact one good way to get noticed is to insti-gate things that enhance the workplace climate. If, for example, you would like more opportunities to socialise with colleagues, organising them can also enhance your career. Not so much because you've taken the initiative, but because you're developing your management skills by taking the lead.

How to enjoy work more

Have you ever wondered why some workplaces are happy and cheerful and others seem filled with glum people? It's often simply because there's more going on than just work, or perhaps it's because everyone looks after the place and it's a nice environment. A lot of it, of course, is down to the people and how they all get on.

We all want to be happy at work, whatever we do and wherever we do it. Here are ten really simple things that can make things more pleasant at work:

10 ways to be happier at work

1. **Pitch your tent** – You need some space to call your own. Even if it's just your corner of the office, get it looking as you want it.

2. **Go green** – Club together with the team and swap the tired spider plants for some large impressive planters. See if your boss will pay half.

3. **Subdue the lights** – Spending your day under the glare of fluorescent strip lights can be depressing. Get some uplighters and desk lights.

4. **Open the window** – Fresh air is good for the brain. Don't sit in a stuffy room, even in midwinter.

5. **Dress for comfort** – If you need to be formally attired for meetings, have a comfy jumper for those long hours alone at your desk.

6. **Take breaks** – Why should it only be the smokers who pop out for five minutes by the back door? Move about and stop for the odd chat.

7. **Accept that we're all different** – Your life plan choices will be showing you how different we all are. Try not to be irritated if others see the world differently.

8. **Build a network** – As well as your formal team, you need an informal support network. Find people you

can collaborate with who will help give you that competitive edge and get things done.

9. **Plan holidays** – There's nothing wrong with having a palm-fringed beach as your screen saver. Unless you've not booked the holiday!

10. **Think positive** – There are two ways to see every situation. Practise seeing the positive rather than the negative. Negativity is highly infectious so keep away from negative people.

Getting things done

Success at work inevitably boils down to getting things done. You can either struggle on your own or become more persuasive and encourage other people to help you. As you are probably getting things done with some vigour in other areas of your life, doing the same at work might even be a little easier!

There are countless experts on human communication. There are also plenty of books expounding clever theories and methodologies. However, effective communication between people is actually remarkably simple if you follow a few basic rules. You need to make sure you clearly explain what you want, why it's important, and when you expect to see it completed. In other words, be sure to say what, when, where, how and why.

Below are ten ways you can win the support of those around you.

10 ways to win the support of other people

1. **Ask** – Too many people hold back from asking. Instead they expect the other person to recognise and seize the opportunity, as if by magic. Take control and ask. If you don't ask, you don't get.

2. **Be explicit** – If you say exactly what you want, you're more likely to get it than if you are confused and unclear.

3. **Win:win** – Others are entitled to ask, 'What's in it for me?' In fact you need to tell them before they ask, then they'll support you.

4. **Big picture** – Failing to complete the task might have global consequences, but if you don't tell the person you've given the task to, they will not appreciate the significance.

5. **Manage expectations** – If something's going to be challenging, say so. Otherwise people will think they're in some way falling short because they find the task difficult.

6. **Trade skills** – This is more than just win:win. It's where you both help each other out, both doing a job you find easy and the other person finds difficult.

7. **Make it competitive** – We all like to win and to win you need some competition. Split tasks and offer a prize for the first to finish.

8. **Nice surprises** – Even small gifts or other tokens of appreciation show that you do appreciate what's been done. Make rewards spontaneous and impulsive as well as formal and organised.

9. **Be helpful yourself** – If you are known for willingly giving your time and expertise, you'll find people receptive when you ask for help.

10. **Say thank you** – It's at the end of the list because you shouldn't need reminding. Sometimes though, we do forget to say thank-you. Don't!

Working for yourself

Working for yourself can liberate you or imprison you. Not everyone enjoys the challenge of self employment, but for many it's the realisation of a lifetime ambition.

If you've had a run of unhappy jobs, or perhaps you think you could do better than your firm, it might be worth giving working for yourself some serious thought as you create your life plan.

Giving up your job to work for yourself is a major decision with major consequences. If it goes well, you will be very happy. If it does not, you might find yourself re-starting the journey from a point further back. This section will help you to explore the opportunity and if it's for you, to create a specific business plan.

10 points to think about when considering self employment

1. Am I just trying to escape from my job? – Hating your job, or even losing it, does not qualify you well for self employment. Facing up to the issues at work will be less traumatic than starting out on your own for the wrong reasons.

2. **Do I worry about money?** – Self employment means no regular salary cheque. Can you handle a haphazard personal cash flow?

3. **Is my family behind me?** – Without the support of your family, you'll never succeed. A business is more demanding than a newborn baby. Make sure everyone understands the sacrifices needed.

4. **What do I enjoy doing?** – There's little point in starting a business to do something you don't enjoy. Working for yourself should be fun.

5. **Is there a demand for what I want to do?** – You need more than a handful of customers. Is there a growing demand for what you want to do?

6. **Could I do it where I am?** – Many firms are happy to diversify. Don't rule out building the business you envisage as a part of your employer's firm. Negotiate performance bonuses.

7. **Can I weather the storm?** – Unless you're very lucky, you'll have no income for the first three to six months.

That's because your business will consume, not generate cash. You need savings.

8. **What about the pension?** – There are lots of hidden benefits to being employed. Appreciate that you'll lose employment benefits.

9. **Do I simply want to get rich?** – Very few successful entrepreneurs become truly rich. Most simply live well and are happy.

10. **Have I really got a choice?** – Sometimes you lose your job and finding another is almost impossible. If this encourages you to go it alone, tread very carefully and read on.

Making the move

Successfully starting and running your own business is one of the most intensely satisfying things you can do in life. However, it's rather like an extreme sport – exhilarating when you win, and painful when you don't.

Millions of people the world over start a business every year. Most are started by just one person, who will be working on their own, at least to start with. Not surprisingly, much research has been done into what makes these people successful. Small businesses form a significant part of the world economy, providing a level of freedom and control that liberates some and would terrify others. If starting up on your own is to form part of your life plan, you want to make sure you stand the best possible chance of success. Here are 10 steps you need to follow.

10 steps to starting your own business

1. **Have a good idea** – Know what you're going to do. Choose something you really understand. This will protect you from many of the risks.

2. **Check out the competition** – See who is already active in your chosen field and work out how you're going to be different.

3. **Do the sums** – How much have you got to invest and live on for the next few months? How much money do you need to get started?

4. **Get advice** – There are a number of Government-funded advice agencies able to offer you independent guidance and support. These are usually funded so you pay little if anything. Do seek advice.

5. **Write a plan** – Write a simple business plan. Many banks provide free templates you can use. Check out the internet or ask your own bank.

6. **Test the market** – Without customers you have no business. Check out potential customers to gauge their interest. Many people find that their current employer becomes their first customer. This is good.

7. **Raise the cash** – Always try to have more money than you need. Borrow first from family and friends. Consider upping the mortgage.

8. **Open the door** – No one ever feels ready to start. However, you'll only effectively iron out the bugs once you start trading.

9. **Watch the pennies** – Spending money is easy and earning it difficult. Don't overspend and make sure you are working profitably.

10. **Measure everything** – Don't get so tied up working in your business that you have no time to work on your business. Stand back and look at what you're doing and record everything.

Work then, in all its forms, is a central part of everyone's life. There are lots of choices, or perhaps lots of challenges to consider. It all depends on where you are and where your life plan says you want to go.

Whatever kind of employment you have, it provides the fuel that keeps the rest of your life on the road. Again, as with your car, it's important to keep the engine, your workplace, tuned and able to deliver the performance you want. Don't forget that most traffic flows two ways; you need to be proactive in managing your work situation as well as reactive to the demands placed upon you.

Making more of leisure time

Your life plan needs to be fun as well as focused. It's as important to plan your leisure time as it is your work time. Your life will become much richer if you widen your range of interests and avoid working 24/7.

When you're not at work, your time is your own. You can relax, enjoy hobbies, take holidays and learn more about the things that interest you. For most of us, leisure time is limited to evenings, weekends and perhaps five weeks' annual leave. That's why it's important to make the best use of your free time.

It's important to recognise that your free time is for you and you alone. It's easy to get led into all kinds of new activities but only do what you instinctively feel is going to be right for you. It's also good to be flexible with your leisure time. Your work life is probably closely scheduled, so retain some freedom to do as you wish at a moment's notice when you're not working.

Hobbies

Hobbies are those things we do because we find them interesting. Some hobbies turn into businesses or careers, but this rarely happens the other way round! For some people, hobbies become an all-consuming lifelong passion. For others, it's more a case of pursuing a succession of passing interests. Which you do will largely depend on your personality. Some people like to explore lots of new things whilst others prefer to drill deep into a specific subject. Your life plan needs to recognise which you are.

Not all hobbies then require a huge commitment. The best ones start with a passing interest that captures your imagination. As you explore the topic, your interest will either deepen or wane. You will either go further or move on. To set you thinking, here are some simple new hobbies you can dip into without great expense. By trying some of these, you will inevitably think of others. It's the process that's important here, rather than the specific examples.

10 simple new hobbies you might explore

1. **Cooking** – If your culinary skills involve moving between freezer and microwave oven, try cooking a meal from scratch. Buying and using fresh ingredients is relaxing and can deliver more wholesome food too. There are lots of recipe websites if you don't want to buy a cookery book!

2. **Gardening** – Are you missing out on the joy of cultivating flowers, shrubs and vegetables? A garden connects you with the earth, literally. Go on, get out in the fresh air!

3. **Get fit** – Getting fit is a great way to spend your spare time. If the gym is too scary, try going for a long walk. All exercise is good for you.

4. **Reading** – You're already doing this aren't you? Why not try some different genres too? Good fiction is more gripping than any movie. You can also join reading clubs where you all read the same volume then discuss it afterwards. This is a great mind stretcher and sociable too.

5. **Music** – Some of us play music, all of us listen to music. If you play, or would like to, why not try lessons? If you listen to music, why not explore some different genres to broaden your range? Music can really surprise you if you let it.

6. **Writing** – Are you a budding novelist? Maybe you're interested in poetry or song lyrics. Why not try creative writing? Like many things, you'll get better with practice. There are countless competitions you can enter and magazines that publish short stories and poems.

7. **Pets** – Rabbits, tropical fish or hamsters are all interesting alternatives to a cat or dog. You might also buy a pedigree animal and show it, or simply take your boisterous new puppy to obedience classes. There are countless pet opportunities to consider. Pets are more than a hobby; they can become members of the family.

8. **Genealogy** – Are you descended from a highwayman or a princess? Have you ever wondered? Why not find out – the internet makes it so much easier to research your family history.

9. **Crafts** – In these days of mass marketing, your friends might really appreciate handmade greetings cards and presents. Making things with your hands, particularly if you work in an office, can be immensely satisfying. Many of the materials you might use, for example pressed flowers and driftwood, are free so creativity need not cost you much at all.

10. **Collect things** – If something catches your eye, or really appeals, how about building a collection? It's a great excuse for going to car boot sales or auctions. What's more, if you tire of your collection, you can usually sell it, sometimes at a profit.

Friends and leisure

Most of the activities listed above can be enjoyed on your own. This is good if you enjoy your own company or perhaps don't have too many people to socialise with at the moment. However, if you want to use your leisure time with friends, you might value some ideas of things to do together. Too often, meeting friends involves spending money. This can mean our social lives being limited by our budget.

Here then are some ideas for low-cost things you can do with friends or family. Use some to get to know your friends better, others to involve elderly relatives at a family gathering.

10 low-cost ways to have fun with friends and family

1. **Parlour games** – Charades is the most obvious example of a game that anyone can play. Why not check out some other traditional games on the internet and put together a themed evening? Parlour games are also great ways to pass time pleasurably with shy or elderly relatives.

2. **Makeovers** – You'll find that many of the party plan companies will gladly organise a free evening's fun for you. Clearly they hope you'll buy some of their products, but that's not compulsory.

3. **Sports day** – Set some sporting challenges that won't embarrass anyone and have a sports evening. Award prizes for the best and most amusing entrant. Try to make sure everyone wins something.

4. **Read a play** – Avoid the dressing up and acting and read a play out loud. All take different parts and record your efforts. Share the resulting MP3 file so that everyone has a copy.

5. **Hire a boat** – If enough of you do it, you'll find you can afford a really big boat. Appoint a captain, cook and crew. If you don't like the water, try paintball or similar. Remember the more of you there are, the less it will usually cost per person.

6. **Dinner party** – Dress up for a formal dinner party. Share the preparation and ask each couple to bring a different course for the meal. Make sure you agree a menu first!

7. **Quiz nights** – Why not form a team and enter local quiz night competitions? Pick friends with a wide range of interests so that no one subject can catch you out.

8. **Dance** – Most people can dance but have you ever thought of trying something new? There are lots of styles of dance you can learn. It's good to take a partner but even more fun if a group of you go. Some places have dance nights where you can learn the steps for free.

9. **Accept a challenge** – Why not try one of the many fundraising challenges available? Some need a team and the best of all need a mix of people with different skills and interests. Some will relish the physical challenge, others the opportunity to play an important supporting role.

10. **Volunteer** – Find something that needs doing and take a load of friends. You could spend a day clearing undergrowth at a nature reserve or redecorating an old folk's day centre. Enjoy working as a team and celebrate your accomplishment with a barbecue or takeaway treat.

What's important about all of these activities is that they can all be repeated. You don't have to do something just once. Over time, you will find that both the group and what you do together will evolve. That's good, because it means your friends have taken a degree of ownership and are adding their own personality to the process. There is a fine line to tread between taking the lead and getting things off the ground and being the person who is expected to do the organising.

Holidays

For most of us, those few weeks of annual leave are the highlight of our year. That quality time away from work will rightly feature highly in your life plan. But what if you can't afford that week on a Greek island? Do you sit at home feeling glum? Decorating the bathroom is perhaps better dealt with over a long weekend than during your two-week summer break.

There are alternative ways to spend your time off work that will leave you equally refreshed and re-energised. Here are some examples:

10 affordable alternatives to a week in the sun

1. **Holiday at home** – Visit all the places you've never bothered with because it's where you live. Eat out every night and use your home like a hotel. Don't do the chores or open the post.

2. **House sit** – Look after someone's pets and plants whilst they are away. Enjoy being somewhere different and again, go out and explore.

3. **House swap** – There are specialist agencies that arrange house swaps. You get to stay in another country for free and so does the person you swap with. You don't need a glamorous home in a popular location either. Home swappers are usually people just like you and me!

4. **Try camping** – Camp sites have hot showers and washing machines these days. It's not as 'back to nature' as you might fear. Tents are cheap and last for years.

5. **Be a carer** – You'll find that many residential homes organise trips away for the people who live there. Why not go with them as a helper and see the world afresh through the eyes of someone else?

6. **Get a job** – If you spend your life indoors, you might welcome two weeks out in the sunshine. Try fruit

picking or being a safety steward at a pop festival. Sometimes a change is better than a rest!

7. **Join a class** – The opportunity to learn a new skill, be it swimming, photography or something more unusual, can be surprisingly cheap. You might find a week-long course you can do without travelling. You'll also meet new people and perhaps make new friends.

8. **Stay with your parents** – The chance to sleep in your old room again gives you a good opportunity to reflect on all you've achieved since you left home. This book has a chapter about parents and ways you can enjoy spending time with them. Why not try it out?

9. **Change your look** – Holidays give you the chance to experiment with every aspect of your appearance. For example, if you're a man, you might grow a beard. Some people even go abroad for aesthetic surgery, although that might not be everyone's idea of affordable.

10. **Empty the cupboards** – It's cold and wet and you don't want to go out. Empty out the cupboards and rediscover things you'd forgotten you had. Change things round and visit lots of shops for inspiration. You don't have to buy anything!

Going on holiday

It's happened. You can finally afford the holiday you really want. How do you make sure the reality lives up to your expectations? How do you minimise the risk of disappointment? Apart from the obvious things like making sure you've got the insurance you need and have had any relevant jabs, there are some really simple, practical things you can do to make your holiday more fun.

10 ways to get more out of your holiday

1. **Plan ahead** – Never be too busy to plan your holiday. Google your destination to see what's going on. Book tickets for things you'll enjoy but might miss if you simply turned up on the night.

2. **Break the journey** – Leaving home at 2am to drive to the airport might save money, but you'll be tetchy for the first few days away. Book a hotel at the airport. Take champagne to drink in the room!

3. **Involve the kids** – Even small children like to play a part in planning activities. Restrict their choice, but let them make choices. It can avoid temper tantrums.

4. **Go native** – Be prepared to try new things. Don't spend all your time beside the pool or on the beach. Gaining an insight into the culture of the country you're visiting will deepen your understanding of your own.

5. **Pace yourself** – Trying to visit every Roman ruin, or every night club, will make your holiday feel like a boot camp. Pace yourself and accept that you won't have time to do everything. Focus on what you want to do most.

6. **Look for ideas** – Different countries do things in different ways. Observe the differences and see if there are things you do at home that could be done differently.

7. **Ask questions** – If something puzzles you, ask someone about it. It's good to be inquisitive and everyone likes it when you show an interest in what they do.

8. **Avoid risks** – Of course you want to enjoy yourself, but spending the next six months in hospital would disrupt your life more perhaps than you'd like. Be sensible, but have a great time too.

9. **Accept the difference** – Some parts of the world are culturally very different to where you live. Accept the difference and don't spend your holiday trying to change things for what you see as the better.

10. **Practice** – The more holidays you have, the more experienced a traveller you'll become. Practice makes perfect!

Learning

Your own time is your own. You don't have to spend it doing things that will benefit your boss. It's time you can fill with whatever you want.

If you are intent on making your life better, then inevitably some of your leisure time will be spent on self development. The kind of self development activities you follow will totally depend on the goals you have set yourself. At first this might seem daunting.

Let's face it, few of us want to return to the disciplined environment of the formal classroom. We want to learn in our own way, at our own pace, and in a way that is appropriate to our ability and interest. The trouble is that once we leave the education system, learning slips down our agenda. We become unaccustomed to study and even reading a book may appear a major challenge.

There's a lot of theory out there about learning styles. This can be confusing, but basically you will have a preferred way to learn. You will learn by seeing, learn by hearing or learn by doing. Of course we don't just follow our preferred method. Imagine for a moment you've just bought a new gadget. Do you open the box and read the manual, or simply take it out, plug it in and experiment? What would your approach be?

Another barrier to learning of any kind is cost. As well as finding the time, most formal learning costs money. As a central theme of the life plan is to introduce you to new opportunities that won't cost money, here are 10 ways to learn that won't cost you a penny.

10 ways to learn for free

1. **Online** – If the internet does not amaze you every single day, you're not using it enough. Visit some university library websites and download their free guides to using search engines. Teach yourself how to find exactly what you're looking for.

2. **On a bus** – Before education was invented, people simply listened to those who already knew. You could learn something from that person beside you on the bus. All you need to do is have a conversation.

3. **At school** – But don't go and sit in a classroom. Get involved in some way helping kids at school. Working with kids can teach you a lot more than it teaches them!

4. **With a friend** – Your best mate is going on a course at work. There are only six people doing it and room for eight. Try inviting yourself along and be surprised at how receptive to the idea people are.

5. **As a volunteer** – Learn strategic management as a charity Trustee or become more assertive by tub-thumping as a fundraiser. Volunteering is a great way to help yourself by helping others.

6. **Because the boss likes you** – Many employers invest in training for their staff that has no relation to their job.

This is because enlightened organisations know that all learning makes you more motivated. Why not enlighten your manager?

7. **By asking why** – Take nothing for granted, question everything.

8. **Government funding** – The UK Government wants everyone to have access to learning. Check out what's available in your town.

9. **Get a mentor** – He or she will help you focus your learning.

10. **Borrow a book** – Start a book circle where you read a book and pass it on. You could do this at work or amongst friends and neighbours.

Throughout this chapter, you have been encouraged to think again about how you spend your leisure time. Because learning is a vital element of any self improvement journey, much here is written to introduce you to the concept that learning can be a leisure pursuit in its own right. It's all about finding the time to try new things, visit new places, meet new people and above all else being inquisitive.

Relationships

Friends, lovers and others we choose to spend our time with enrich our lives and in many ways make us feel part of something bigger than ourselves. It's too easy to feel left out of things if you're sitting alone surrounded by groups of people having a great time.

Almost every aspect of your life plan will involve other people. How you relate to them and, more importantly, how you feel about yourself is vital to your success.

Meeting new people

Almost all relationships start in the same way. You meet someone new, perhaps as an introduction, and something connects. As you find out more about each other, the relationship might evolve into a friendship or a romance.

You almost certainly already have a circle of friends. But because you spend your time with them, it can be difficult to widen your circle of friends and meet new people. However, widening your circle of friends will widen your understanding of the world. We learn so much from other people that in many ways you cannot know enough people. The only limit to your personal network of friends should be the time you have to keep in touch with them all!

Here then are some tips for those times when you're not with a group and would like to meet some new people. Remember that you then have the choice as to whether you introduce them to your existing friends or simply have a number of separate friendships.

10 ways to widen your circle of friends

1. **Break the ice** – You know how you meet the same person at the station every morning, nod, smile but don't have a conversation? Find a way to break the ice and find out about them. Sit together on the train and discuss common interests.

2. **Start a lunchtime club** – Does everyone eat sandwiches at their desk? Why not start some lunchtime clubs at work? Put invitations on the notice boards and see who turns up. Make the theme something really interesting, to you and to others.

3. **Find other new people** – Perhaps you're new in town and don't know many people. Find others who have just moved in and explore together. You'll either become friends or find new friends together.

4. **Online** – There are an increasing number of online social networks. They enable you to post a profile and exchange views with others who share your interests. Online networks are fantastic when you want to find people who share some obscure interest with you.

5. **Friends of friends** – People who know you need little encouragement to introduce you to the people they know. Your social circle should constantly be growing, spinning out new circles as the group becomes too large and unwieldy.

6. **At the coffee machine** – Many friendships start at work. This is often because you have time to get to know each other over time. It helps that you have work in common; it gives you a topic to talk about!

7. **Dig out old friends** – Do you ever wonder what happened to your best friends at school? The internet can help you find them again. But don't assume you'll get on, even though you probably will.

8. **Networking events** – From speed dating to business breakfasts, there are lots of organised networking events you can attend. You might attend because of your work, but may meet someone you'd like to socialise with too.

9. **Join things** – Gyms and clubs are places where you'll meet new people. You also have a common interest or you both wouldn't be there.

10. **Be receptive** – People will also see you as someone they'd like to know better. Make time for them and find out if you've much in common.

Being a good friend

Good friends are hard to find. When you have a good friend, you know you are never going to be alone. You have someone to share your news with, both good and bad; someone who will support you through the tough patches and help you celebrate your achievements. These are the special people you cannot live without, who make you feel valued and part of something special. They may be your partner, or they may not. They will certainly know you better than your mum and perhaps that's the acid test!

If you have good friends, you will already know how important they are. But ask yourself this. How good a friend are you to them? It's easy to enjoy the benefits but of course

to be good friends takes two. You have to sometimes put your own needs to one side and insist on being a good friend in return.

When you're with good friends, you want to do special things, things that are memorable and perhaps have more meaning than the usual drink in a bar. Here are some ideas to inspire you.

10 fun things you can do with good friends

1. **Climb a mountain** – It need not be a high mountain, but because you can trust good friends more, you won't mind taking more risks when they are there to support you. Try new things with those really good friends and you'll become even closer.

2. **Hire a castle** – Find a 20 bedroomed castle and organise a week-long party with a large group of friends. Choose somewhere with staff so you don't need to do the washing up.

3. **Fancy dress party** – Organise a party and play silly games. If it's only your friends, no one is likely to get embarrassed!

4. **Karaoke** – Club together and buy a karaoke machine and take it in turns to sing your favourite songs. This is supposed to be embarrassing, but everyone takes part so it's fun all the same.

5. **A day at the races** – Go with a friend, or perhaps a group of you can hire a hospitality suite and do it in real style.

6. **Take over the pub** – If there are enough of you to fill a room, then fill a bar. Why not meet every Monday when things are quiet and you might have the place to yourselves?

7. **See the world** – Travelling alone is far less fun than travelling with a friend. Go with one close friend or take a group and hire a villa. There are endless opportunities, all better than a holiday on your own.

8. **Kids' games** – Great for those warm summer afternoons. Play children's games and if enough of you have children, get them to play as well!

9. **Learn a new language** – Doing this with a friend or two gives you someone to practise with. It also makes giving up harder.

10. **Share a classic sports car** – Club together and buy your dream car. Organise a rota so that you all have your chance to drive it.

Making friendships closer

It can be quite upsetting when friendships weaken as interests diverge. In many ways, this is inevitable in a long-term relationship. Sometimes it's best to accept that you've both changed and move on. At others, you may want to strengthen the relationship (particularly if it's your current life partner!).

10 tips to help improve any relationship

1. **Put them first** – After all, this relationship is important to you. Work, acquaintances and solitary pursuits should take second place to the people who really matter in your life.

2. **Make space** – It is important to allow people some freedom. It's healthy to have interests and friendships that are unique to one or other of you. Remember that the experiences unique to each person enrich the bond between you.

3. **Trust each other** – Suspicion can undermine a relationship. Be open, trusting and honest with each other. Discuss concerns and differences of opinion.

4. **Value each other's work** – If your job pays twice that of your friend's or partner's, it doesn't make it twice as important. We all have different abilities and different goals. Respect individuality.

5. **Forgive and move on** – We all make mistakes. Don't let them spoil an otherwise brilliant relationship.

6. **Adapt over time** – We all change as the years pass. Recognise that you might need to introduce new ideas and activities and let others slip. Don't try to cling to the things you both used to do if only you want to continue.

7. **Do your chores** – Always do your share of those mundane tasks. Don't let the other person do the dirty work every time.

8. **Admit mistakes** – The feelings of guilt associated with a 'moment of madness' can erode a relationship like acid. Admit your mistakes and seek forgiveness. Learn from them too.

9. **Remember anniversaries** – If you habitually forget those important dates, write them down where you'll be reminded.

10. **Say that you care** – It's so easy to take someone for granted, especially if you've been together for many years. Old couples and old friends can both be guilty for forgetting to say that they care. Make a point of telling those important to you that they are!

Repairing relationships

All relationships have their ups and downs. The most important thing to remember when things are going badly is that it takes two people to argue; it also takes two people to make up. In other words, relationships are all about communication.

If a relationship is beginning to suffer, talking about it is often the best way to resolve the issue. This can be difficult as the fear of breaking up may inhibit one or both from speaking their mind. Open, non-judgemental conversation can go a long way towards resolving the issues that are causing the rift. Sometimes it's easier to write things down, perhaps even email each other, than to try to resolve your difference of opinion face to face.

Sometimes a relationship is damaged beyond repair, or particularly with friendships, has run its natural course. If you're not the one prompting the end of any relationship, it's natural to feel hurt and abandoned. Here are some tips that might help when this happens to you.

10 ways to cope when any relationship ends

1. **Try to keep talking** – If there is stuff to resolve, it's easier if you keep talking. However, once you've settled any outstanding business, let the other person go. They, like you, need to live their life.

2. **Understand why** – If you know the real reasons for the split, you can deal with it better. Even when casual acquaintances start to give you the cold shoulder, it can be hurtful if you don't know why.

3. **Don't blame yourself** – What's happened has happened and you can't turn back the clock. Focus on your future, not the past.

4. **Get out and about** – Don't sit at home and mope. You have other friends don't you? Spend time with them, but don't bore them with your problems.

5. **Be practical** – If it's a relationship that's ended, try to separate the emotional trauma from the practical issues. Don't make shared possessions weapons in a war of retribution.

6. **Don't change too much else** – If you've lost your squash partner, you now have Wednesday evenings free. Don't get so upset that you stop going out on the other nights as well. Keep things in perspective.

7. **Let go and move on** – You have to accept the inevitable sometimes. The sooner you recognise that it's over, the sooner you can plug that gap in your life.

8. **Take a break** – Sometimes it's good to go away for a day or two to reflect on the relationship. Are there things to learn for the future?

9. **Make a list** – Write down all the good things you have done together. None of it might have happened had you never met. Celebrate what was good.

10. **You're not alone** – There are very few people who have never had a relationship end. That means that others will know what it feels like, so you know you're not alone. It's OK to seek a little solace from people you trust who may have had the same experience.

Neighbours

Because neighbours live close to you, they can be as important as friends, even if you don't get on. You can choose your friends but your neighbours are either there already or arrive without you being able to do anything about it.

Neighbours can do much to make life easier and more enjoyable. Conversely, a poor relationship with your neighbours can make life very unpleasant indeed. You probably nod and say hello to quite a few people who live nearby, but the challenge is to find a way to get to know them better. In fact good neighbours can also become good friends, although that too has its risks. Unless you live in the middle of the country, surrounded by fields, neighbours will play a key role in your happiness and thus your ability to realise your ambitions.

10 ways to meet your neighbours

1. **Host a party** – Take the initiative and invite everyone round for a party. Keep it low key and informal. You simply want people to meet each other and talk. Good ideas are bound to emerge.

2. **Cut the grass** – If they're away for a week, offer to cut their grass and keep an eye on their home. They'll probably invite you round to say thanks.

3. **Share things** – If you're hiring a carpet cleaner, see who else might like to use it over the same weekend. There are lots of things neighbours can share.

4. **Baby-sit** – Find others with children and start a baby-sitting circle. Everyone benefits and everyone probably goes out more often!

5. **Feed pets** – Offer to feed next door's cat when they are away for the night. Remember you need to make the first move, don't wait to be asked. If you feed their pet first, you won't feel bad asking if they'd mind looking after yours when you're away.

6. **Accept deliveries** – Waiting in for stuff to be delivered is a pain. So is waiting for plumbers and maintenance people to arrive; they're often late. If you're at home all day, offer to sign for parcels.

7. **Start a campaign** – If you are concerned about planned developments or other changes to your neighbourhood, others will be too. Knock on everyone's door to canvass opinion. Encourage people to make their feelings known to those making the decisions that affect you all.

8. **Neighbourhood Watch** – Your local council or police can show you how to do this. Everyone joins in and reports any suspicious activity to the authorities. Neighbourhood Watch schemes reduce crime. Start one.

9. **Do the shopping** – If you notice that someone is ill and housebound, offer to do their shopping. Invite other neighbours to help out as well.

10. **Just say hello** – If none of these ideas appeals to you, simply go up to your neighbour and say; 'Hello, I've been meaning to introduce myself for some time now . . .'

Dealing with problems

Rather like your workplace, your neighbourhood is populated by people you have not chosen. In other words, unlike your friends, you won't get on with everyone all of the time. Your life plan will probably focus on building friendships, but it also needs to contain tips on what to do when you and a neighbour no longer see eye to eye.

10 neighbour problems and how to overcome them

1. Noisy parties – If your party is going to disturb the neighbours, invite them to join in the fun. If it's their party, consider gate-crashing!

2. **Tall hedges** – Always mention this casually before marching round to complain. Hedges grow slowly; so too should any resulting dispute.

3. **Banging doors** – If your neighbour is just a wall's width away, you may hear banging doors and worse. Ask them if they can hear you and agree tactics to minimise the nuisance.

4. **Dog poo** – If everyone seems to let their dog use your front lawn as a toilet, consider planting a low-growing prickly border hedge. Alternatively, a small sign and supply of polythene bags might help.

5. **Rowdy children** – You have to accept that children make noise, especially when playing out in the garden. Put the paddling pool close to your back door, not at the bottom of the garden where it's close to someone else's windows. If your neighbour's kids are disturbing you, mention it to their parents when you next see them.

6. **Revving engines** – We all have to go to work. Is your neighbour simply waking you up when they start the

car, or are they actually spending Sunday afternoon tuning the engine? Recognise the difference and tolerate what is unavoidable.

7. **Stigma** – If you're suffering prejudice or abuse from neighbours, a good first step is to seek advice from your faith or other community group. There will hopefully be some local success stories you can learn from. Equally, question in your own mind if your feelings about some neighbours are fair, or founded in some deep-rooted prejudice.

8. **Lewd behaviour** – If it's being staged for you to observe, your neighbour may need professional help. If it's just that you're looking over the fence, try looking somewhere else. Try not to make a big deal of it unless you feel intimidated.

9. **Vermin** – Some pets, particularly poultry, can attract rats and mice. Your council can deal with vermin in your garden and will also go next door.

10. **Crime** – If you suspect your neighbour is breaking the law, it's for your own moral values to decide if you should ignore or report it. Be realistic and tolerant if they seem to have different values to you. Remember it's costly to move house, so you don't want to fall out with the people next door.

The people around you, be they friends, family or simply the people next door, have a huge impact on your ability to achieve the things you want. That's why your relationship with them needs to be as good as possible. The more people you have supporting you in your quest to make life better, the better life will become – for you and for them.

Children

One of the biggest decisions you can make in your life is whether or not to have children. There are many factors that influence that decision, not least the views of your partner. (And there are also people who choose to have children without a partner.)

Even if you decide not to become a parent, it's likely you will have friends who will have children. We all therefore spend some time with children, even if they are not our own. It makes sense as you develop your life plan to explore how to make that time enjoyable and valuable for all concerned.

Parenthood: yes or no?

Once you become a parent, you're a parent for life. Children are a major commitment, financially, emotionally and in terms of your freedom to do as you please. On the other hand, they can become the central focus of your life plan when they're young and also during their adult years.

Few take the decision lightly, although for some it just happens and the pregnancy is a big surprise. In fact unplanned families can turn out to be the happiest! If you are at the point in your life where you are contemplating starting a family, here are some questions to ask yourself.

10 questions to ask when considering starting a family

1. **Is it just instinct?** – We are pre-programmed to want children. It's nature at work. Having a family then can make you feel you are doing what is natural. Try listing the pros and cons and balance instinct with the practical points you need to consider.

2. **Are parents pressing?** – Sometimes your parents' desire to become grandparents is greater than your desire to be a parent. Don't let their ambitions prejudice your own decision. Ask them how they can help if you do decide to have children.

3. **Are you ready for a career break?** – Having a baby means take maternity leave. Many couples also decide to then work part-time and share childcare responsibilities. How does it fit with your career plans?

4. **Can you afford it?** – Raising a child is expensive. Look long and hard at your finances and work out how you'll manage. It might be better to wait and try to save, or you might decide to go ahead and manage somehow. There is no right answer.

5. **Have we got room?** – Is your home suitable for children? If it's a one-bedroom studio flat, you might consider trading up first. How far are you from schools and other facilities you'll need? You will look for different things from your neighbourhood when you have children.

6. **How strong is your relationship?** – Some people have children to repair an ailing relationship but this doesn't always work. Ask yourselves if you're ready to commit to perhaps 20 years together as parents. It's a big question.

7. **Will it be easy?** – Getting pregnant is as difficult for some as it is easy for others. Be prepared for it to take some time to happen, and don't become anxious if it takes longer than you'd hoped. Have you the stamina for what might be a long haul?

8. **Is life just too good to change?** – If you're really enjoying life, have a great job and a full social life, a baby might change things more than you'd like. It's not selfish to remain childless; it's your choice.

9. **What about twins?** – If one of your parents is a twin, there's a chance you'll have twins too. Many fertility treatments also lead to multiple births. Could you handle having two babies when you planned only one?

10. **Do the genes fit?** – Some people decide to remain childless because they might potentially pass on some genetic condition. If this is you, take professional advice before committing yourself either way.

Raising children

If you have children, you'll want the best for them. That may not necessarily mean giving them the same kind of upbringing you had. Times change and there are more opportunities today than when you were a child. Your life plan needs to accommodate your wish to be a good parent, but without sacrificing your other ambitions. Here are some top parenting tips.

10 top parenting tips

1. **Show them you love them** – Fathers in particular can find it difficult to cuddle and kiss their children. However, children need physical comfort from both parents. Let the children see you cuddle each other too.

2. **Maintain boundaries** – Children need to know what's acceptable and what's not. However liberal you are, make sure you define and protect the boundaries of tolerable behaviour.

3. **Listen** – Even babies vocalise a wide range of feelings and demands. Older children learn by asking questions. Make time to listen.

4. **Tired kids sleep longer** – Exercise is good for us all, particularly the young. If your child is constantly on the go, take him or her to the park and play ball. Encourage them to play sport.

5. **Keep your cool** – Don't let your little darlings wind you up. Getting heated won't help them understand what they're doing wrong.

6. **Spare the rod** – If you're over 40, the chances are your parents and perhaps teachers hit you when you were naughty. Psychologists now believe this gives out all the wrong messages. Impose sanctions instead.

7. **Don't criticise** – Self esteem is fragile in the young and easily damaged. Criticise bad behaviour but don't criticise the child.

8. **Give them space** – The older a child gets, the more they'll value their own private space. If you're worried by what you might find, don't poke about their room.

9. **Apologise** – If you get it wrong, apologise. No one is perfect and parents should not always be right.

10. **Involve your own parents** – They managed to raise you didn't they? So why not make sure your children build strong relationships with all of their grandparents.

Quality time with children

The list above helps you develop a mutually respectful relationship with your children. However, there is more to parenting than that. If you have children, or perhaps are close to people who do, you will want to spend quality time with the children.

How you define quality time will depend on your own vision and values. Quality doesn't necessarily mean educational; it can mean a whole lot more. It's also about planning your own life to leave time for the children. At times you'll need to park them in front of the TV and get on with something else. At other times, you'll want to do things together that are much more exciting. Here are some tips to help you do that.

10 ways to spend quality time with children

1. **Make a date** – Children like routine, so why not set aside one afternoon a week when you do something special together?

2. **Share the planning** – Get the children to decide what you're going to do at least some of the time. Make time to plan and discuss what you're all going to do. Anticipation can be as much fun as the activity.

3. **Play** – When did you last play with your children? It's almost too obvious, but it enables you to enter their world where they're in charge and know what to do.

4. **Create a gang** – Sometimes it might be good to do something with another family. See if you can create a gang from amongst your friends and theirs to share the occasional expedition.

5. **Buy a season ticket** – This encourages you to make regular return visits to a favourite place, perhaps the zoo. It's good to see how places change over time. You also see more when you go somewhere regularly.

6. **Share a hobby** – Some things, for example photography, horse riding or fishing, can be shared. Choose pastimes where the children can do better than the adults!

7. **Cook a meal** – It's always useful to learn to cook. However, cooking a meal together is also a great way to

work together on something. You can then celebrate your successes by eating them.

8. **Be competitive** – Work together to win things. They could be quizzes, competitions, races and more. Have the children find the opportunities and be brave enough to try some things you would normally avoid.

9. **Dig out your old school reports** – Children are fascinated by evidence that adults were once children too. School reports, photos and other memories from your past will enable you to discuss both your past and their future.

10. **Press flowers** – This is just one example of the things children used to do that you can try together. Look up traditional pastimes and give some a try.

Childcare

Raising children is an important part of many people's lives, but should not completely take over. Make time for yourself and continue to work towards your other life plan goals. Sacrificing ambition for children sounds laudable, but can leave you resenting the opportunities you feel your children have denied you.

You need to have a life as well, so will want to delegate childcare at times to someone else. When choosing childcare, perhaps for the time when you are going to be at work, always visit the provider a few times to see how they manage the facility. Usually, it will either feel right or it won't. Don't ignore your instinct and also ask your child for his or her opinion. Finally, talk to parents who already have their children cared for there. Listen to their views and see how they fit with your own perception.

Encouraging children to achieve

In time, your children, or those you care about, will set their own life goals. First they probably need to experience something of the world and mature a little. It is very tempting to help them out by suggesting some ambitions that you think they'll like. This though can have the opposite effect as at times, rebellion will be their preferred response.

There is a balance to be struck between suggestion and support. Creating opportunities for them will usually achieve far more than simply telling them what you would do if you were them.

I want to be an astronaut when I grow up.
OK son, let's draw up a plan.

10 ways to nurture ambition in children

1. **Encourage them** – Someone's got to be Prime Minister. If your child wants to do something remarkable, don't rubbish the idea. Encourage them to work out how they could make it happen.

2. **Challenge them** – Wrapping your child in cotton wool will only make the world seem more frightening than it really is. Set them challenges that will stretch them. Celebrate the successes with them.

3. **See the world** – Give your children opportunities to see new things, new places and meet new people. No one changed the world by stopping at home. Take them travelling.

4. **Buy books** – OK, so it's natural for an author to recommend buying books. Reading broadens the mind and inspires ambition; buy books.

5. **Encourage heroes** – There's nothing wrong with hero worship, in fact it's a brilliant way to focus ambition. Encourage children to find out how their heroes did what they did and how it all started.

6. **Role play** – Creative play develops creative thinking. Children do this instinctively, but encourage them and suggest scenarios for them to explore.

7. **Group play** – Children grow up to be more confident if they regularly play with other children. They also learn how to influence others.

8. **Accept change** – If yesterday's budding astronaut becomes today's budding airline pilot, don't scoff. It could simply be that your child has been thinking and recognises that flying a plane is more achievable.

9. **It's not about money** – Don't push your child towards high-earning careers. There's more to life than money.

10. **Anything is possible** – Each and every person is unique and today the world is more egalitarian than ever before. Almost anything is possible if you want to do it badly enough. Don't discourage ambition.

Children are important to us all, whether or not we are parents. They form the next generation and so inevitably will have an increasing influence over our lives as we grow older. We all have the opportunity to make a positive contribution to the lives of young people. The extent to which we do so will be dictated by our individual life plans.

Parents

Parents often find it difficult to let go of their child, even though it means welcoming a much loved adult into their lives. Equally, as you establish your own life, you will want to let them closer to you again. We all create distance between ourselves and our parents as we grow up. You now need to establish a different kind of relationship with your parents. If they are growing old, you may find them seeking your advice and help with their life choices. This too can be difficult for you both, as the roles will effectively have reversed from when you were younger.

We cannot change our parents but we can influence our relationship with them. It might be good to take a look at how you get on with your parents as you build your life plan. You will almost inevitably remain important to them for all of their lives. Perhaps you'd like to feel the same way about them.

How the relationship changes

There's a pretty fundamental piece of psychology that will help you manage your parents effectively. It's called 'transactional analysis' and it explains a lot about how you and your parents interact. It's used a lot in relationship counselling. This is because it enables you to change the way someone relates to you, by changing your style of approach to them. Here is a simple explanation:

There are three states:

- Parent – authoritative, nurturing, dominant
- Child – obedient, demanding, submissive
- Adult – mature, responsible, equal

Your relationship with your parents will have started, not surprisingly, as a parent:child one. They were always right because you were young and did not know much. As you grow up, you push at this, which inevitably leads to tension and perhaps even conflict. If you behave as a 'difficult child', your simply push your parents further into parent mode. That's why it's so important to remain rational and not to respond emotionally when your parents try to parent you when you're grown up.

Getting closer to your parents

You life plan may include getting closer to your parents. There is more chance that if they understand what you are doing, in terms of taking control of your life and your future, they will be more supportive. At least they will have that opportunity! Your parents will always be your parents, but there are many other roles they can fulfil if you choose to help them see the opportunities.

10 ways to show your parents that you're now grown up

1. **Treat them as adults** – Don't defer as you did as a child, but treat them as adults and they'll do the same to you. Respond to them rationally and not emotionally. Let them see you as other adults do.

2. **Talk to them often** – The more you tell them about your life, your hopes, your fears and your challenges,

the less they'll have to guess. Parents who guess are usually parents who worry.

3. **Make the first move** – Raise controversial topics with them yourself. It saves them the embarrassment and, when discussed, will probably put their minds at rest. Remember that if they have concerns, others may share them.

4. **Discuss current affairs** – Demonstrate that you have views and debate your differences of opinion. Gently challenge the view they hold that you disagree with. Help them see things from your perspective.

5. **Keep them young** – You getting older means they're getting old. Help them make the most of where they are. Treat them to new experiences and challenge them to try new things.

6. **Kiss your mum** – Parents miss physical contact with their children. There's nothing wrong with a son hugging his dad either. Show them love.

7. **Accept their experience** – Whilst times change, issues don't. It's not belittling your maturity to seek and listen to your parents' advice. Chances are, they've encountered almost the same problem.

8. **Pick up the tab** – Parents always pay for their kids. Adult kids should sometimes pay for their parents. It reminds them you're independent.

9. **Tolerate fixations** – Perhaps you're happily single and they want you hitched. Accept their fixation as a genuine concern and help them to see that you're happy as you are. Parents can fixate on really odd things!

10. **Involve your children** – Being a grandparent gives them a chance to organise children without organising you.

However busy your life, you could probably allow time to visit your parents and spend some time with them. If you seek to establish, or perhaps strengthen, your adult:adult relationship with your parents, you will need to lead the conversation and broach subjects that perhaps have not been broached before. Here are some you might like to try.

10 questions that will get your parents talking more openly

1. **Tell me about your family** – Every family has its secrets, its black sheep and its heroes. Encourage your parents to share these stories. You might even write them down.

2. **Tell me why** – You are bound to have unanswered questions from your childhood. Explore those half-forgotten memories and understand why things were as they were. Be prepared to accept and move on.

3. **Where's the will?** – No one likes to write their will but it's far easier than dying without one. Sensitively raise the subject. Make sure you know where they keep this and other valuable documents.

4. **Who was this?** – Go through the old family photos and have your parents put names and dates on the back. This process will prompt them to remember and share fascinating facts from their past. Create a family archive.

5. **Were you a campaigner?** – Find out what issues your parents felt strongly about in their youth. Did they campaign for what is now accepted as normal? Explore with them how attitudes have changed over the years and what this means to you and your life plan.

6. **How did you meet?** – Sharing the story of their romance will trigger other tales from your parents'

young lives. What were their parents' attitudes to the relationship? Gain an insight into the relationship.

7. **What have been the highlights of your life?** – Encourage the celebration of past successes. Compare your parents' achievements with your own life goals.

8. **What have been the low points of your life?** – Find out about how your parents dealt with any challenges they faced. Your resilience may well be influenced by theirs.

9. **What do you still want to achieve in your life?** – Although most will reply modestly, press a little and unearth dreams you can help make true. You'll find there is no age limit to ambition.

10. **What changes in the world have surprised you most?** – Explore how politics, prejudices and practices have changed. Discuss how they continue to change. Compare aspects of your life with theirs.

Family history

As you work through your own life plan, you may be creating the family history that future generations will find inspiring. Equally, you may be able to take encouragement from your own family's past achievements, even if they are modest, or even greater, when compared with your own.

Few people could read until two hundred years ago. Before then tradition, history and culture were passed down the generations by word of mouth. Storytelling was used extensively to inform and guide each generation, building on the experience of those who had gone before. Exploring your family's history may help you to understand the starting point for your own life plan. For example, the sayings, prejudices and traditions your parents hold dear may have been picked up from their parents and so forth.

You may also discover particularly interesting ancestors who can provide valuable reference points for your life plan. These could be people who achieved great things, or perhaps people who became notorious for other reasons! It can be useful to look back at a time when you are also planning ahead.

Old age

Just as you were once totally dependent on your parents, so as they age, they will become increasingly dependent on you. This can be a joy or an enormous burden. Here are some ways to help them, without compromising your plans.

10 tips for helping your parents as they grow old

1. **Borrow their slippers** – The hopefully gradual physical decline of old age can be very depressing. Imagine what you'll feel like when it happens to you. It will help you understand how they feel.

2. **Encourage experimenting** – Older people focus too often on what's no longer achievable. Get them to try new things you know *are* possible.

3. **Agree the ground rules** – If you don't want them to ring you every evening for a chat, suggest a time and frequency you can both live with.

4. **Accept the gifts** – At times, old people seem desperate to give stuff away. Accept their gifts but be prepared to return them later if necessary.

5. **Keep them moving** – Even though the joints might creak and they can no longer run, it's important to keep them mobile. Mobile = independent.

6. **Don't take bribes** – You might like the idea of your parents buying you a big house so you can all live together. After 20 years though, it might not be so much fun. Beware of those bribes!

7. **Ignore emotional blackmail** – It's tough, but just because they wiped your bottom when you were a baby, you don't need to nurse them when they're old.

Help out by all means, but don't be bullied into becoming their carer, unless that forms part of your own life plan.

8. **Hear it again** – Old age is a time when favourite anecdotes and stories are shared time and time again. You need to be patient and let them tell you the same stories again and again.

9. **Answers to ultimate questions** – Your aging parents will be more aware of their own mortality than they have ever been before. Dying is a scary prospect; encourage them to explore their faith if they have one.

10. **Lost some marbles** – Remember that the brain fades in old age. They might not understand how demanding they're becoming.

Grandparents

If you have both children and parents, then your children have grandparents. It's obvious, but too often as we seek to maintain a healthy distance between our parents and our lives, we overlook the huge benefits of encouraging your parents to be active grandparents. Sharing your children's upbringing with your parents can enrich the life of all three generations. It can also free up time for you to realise other ambitions. There's nothing wrong with asking your parents to take the children on the days you want to do something that's just for you.

Your parents' life plan

You'll probably have more time to achieve your own ambitions if your parents stay healthy, active and engaged with the world. Older people can become quite demanding when they begin to feel vulnerable or unwell. It helps nobody when old people become withdrawn and lose interest. Here are ten things you can encourage your parents to do.

10 new things you can encourage parents to do

1. **Travel** – They now have the time, maybe the money and there are many places to see that years ago were inaccessible. Get them abroad!

2. **Sports** – Keeping fit keeps you alive longer. Some sports are almost exclusively played by old people, for example bowls. Get them playing.

3. **Writing** – Is your mum a budding poet? Or perhaps your dad might like to write his autobiography? Publication doesn't matter; you're the reader.

4. **Pets** – Pampering a pet stops them pestering you. If they buy a dog, it also encourages them to take long walks and keep fit.

5. **Shop** – Older people have a habit of making do with what they have rather than buying new things. Encourage your parents to go shopping and treat themselves from time to time.

6. **Volunteer** – Old people have experience and time. There's always someone older or worse off whom they can help. Charities need volunteers.

7. **Join** – You'd be amazed how many clubs and societies there are. Whatever their interest, there's a club or society for them.

8. **Surf** – The internet is a great place to explore. There are even senior chat-rooms where they can meet fellow enthusiasts online.

9. **Learn** – You should never stop learning. Perhaps a foreign language to help with those holidays or a new craft or skill.

10. **Love** – If your parents are still together, then old age brings both opportunities and challenges. Encourage them to revisit romance.

Your parents raised you and will take an interest in your life as it evolves. Sharing your life plan with them, as well as encouraging them to make their own plans, will help stop them worrying about you. Being proactive in managing your relationship with your parents will reassure them, bring them closer to you, and might just make your life plan easier to achieve.

Money

It would be impossible to create a life plan that did not involve money. We all need money to cover our living expenses, unless that is you've already made, or perhaps inherited enough money to be truly comfortable! Maintaining and perhaps growing income, together with reducing any burden of debt, is for most people one of the central themes of their life plan.

How much money do you need?

Enough is always a little more than you have. Very few can claim to be comfortably off. Most of us manage our finances month by month, trying to keep on top of the bills and save a little for the future.

Furthermore, many of our ambitions will cost money to achieve. You cannot, for example, fly a plane without first taking expensive lessons. There are many costly temptations placed in front of us. The answer is to balance common sense with indulgence. In other words, you need to strike a happy and affordable medium, between being miserly and saying yes to everything.

Here are 10 money temptations and how to handle them.

10 reasons why you've never got enough

1. **You want nice things** – You want to do well and our society defines your success by the things that you own. There is no shortage of things you can buy. Make buying nice things a goal and avoid those impulse buys.

2. **You'd rather not wait** – Whilst our grandparents saved up for things, we choose to have them now and pay off a loan. We're too impatient to save, and credit has never been more freely available. Set yourself a credit target and don't exceed it.

3. **We're all collectors** – Once you've started acquiring things, you yearn for things to go with them. Buy a sofa and then you need a new carpet. Pace yourself.

4. **Envy** – We all want to keep up with our neighbours, family and colleagues at work. Once one buys a new gadget, we all want one. Why not share some of them rather than have one each?

5. **Advertising works** – Those marketers write words and create images that tug at our wallet and encourage us to spend what we haven't got. Don't be led into thinking that you're the only person left without that 'must have' commodity.

6. **Socialising is expensive** – No one wants to sit at home alone every evening. A night out with friends costs

money, but who wants to be the party pooper and suggest you go somewhere cheaper? Introduce some occasional 'low cost' fun evenings to your social network.

7. **Children** – If you have children, you'll know that they're expensive to rear. They also always want you to buy them the latest toy. Don't give in too easily.

8. **Romance** – If your relationship is new or perhaps going through a sticky patch, it makes sense to invest in romantic gifts and experiences. Try to go Dutch rather than go overboard. Remember, it's you they're really interested in, not what you buy for them.

9. **Addiction** – Perhaps a tough word to use, but we can become addicted to all kinds of things. Drink, drugs and tobacco are well-known expensive habits, but what about those lattes and cappuccinos? They cost lots too.

10. **You earn too little** – A good way to justify over-expenditure is to blame it on a shortage of income. You need to work on both sides of that equation.

Get rich quick

The world is full of get-rich-quick schemes. They are often promoted by people who are not rich themselves, but seem able to convince others that they know the secret. In truth there are no quick ways to get rich. If you want to increase your income, it usually involves working longer hours or perhaps finding a better paid job. Perhaps you can learn new skills that will enable you to earn more or even find a second income of some kind.

Be wary of get-rich-quick schemes of any kind. Ask yourself why the person promoting it needs to encourage you to join in. If it's that good, why do they need you?

Spending less

However much you earn, there never seems to be quite enough money to last the month. Very few people can claim to have all the money they need. There are simple ways you can reduce your monthly spending without necessarily going without. Here are ten to get you started.

10 simple ways to spend less

1. **Check direct debits** – Are you really sure you know what's leaving your bank account every month? Insurance premiums for no longer needed policies and subscriptions to organisations we no longer support can trickle out of your bank unnoticed for years.

2. **Consolidate debt** – Mortgages are cheaper than credit card debt. Independent Financial Advisers can help you reduce your outgoings by rolling all your debt into a mortgage. Always take advice though!

3. **Collect coins** – Small change just disappears. Make checking your pockets or purse for 50p coins a habit and save them in a jar.

4. **Bulk buy** – Whilst large packs usually represent better value at the supermarket, your challenge is to avoid the temptation to use more when you get home because you have more.

5. **Share with neighbours** – Why buy a new hedge-trimmer when you can borrow your neighbour's? In return, let them use your electric drill. Consider setting up a 'tool pool' in your street.

6. **Leave your credit card at home** – Harsh perhaps, but if you habitually impulse buy, this will stop you! You can always go back.

7.   **Give pocket money** – Giving the children a weekly allowance means they can buy things themselves. If they run out of money midweek, they'll learn to be more frugal, rather than just asking you for more!

8.   **Be nice to your parents** – As parents become older, they are more likely to use their own spare cash to indulge their hard-up offspring.

9.   **Take a flask** – Have you ever added up how much cash you spend in coffee bars? Unless visiting them is part of your social or work routine, taking a flask of coffee or tea will save you lots.

10. **Buy second hand** – Search for bargain buys in charity shops and at auction websites. Almost everything you need can be bought second hand. Take a look around.

Budgeting

One of the arts of managing your expenditure is to set a budget. You can make it as detailed or as straightforward as you wish. What's important is to begin to monitor what you spend, so unless you're really determined, keep it simple! You can use a notebook or spreadsheet to record:

- Your fixed monthly outgoings
- Your regular household bills
- Subscriptions and membership fees
- Food and other living expenses
- What you spend on leisure and entertainment

You might need to check your bank statements and credit card bills to work all this out. If there are costs you can't identify, well done. You might be close to killing an unnecessary expense!

The difference between your income and necessary expenditure is the amount you can save or spend on fun. You must decide if you want to save or spend any spare cash you have each month.

Saving

It's not very fashionable to save money these days. However, budgeting to build a small 'rainy day' fund is always a good idea. It means that you can cope with minor crises without panic or problem.

If you really get the saving habit, or perhaps you're fortunate to have some spare cash, there are real benefits to be had, apart that is from any interest the money earns you. You can, for example, negotiate discounts on some of the things you might buy, rather than paying interest on a loan.

Savings do need to work for you. There is so much choice of investment vehicles, from high interest accounts to shares and much more. If you have a sizeable amount to put away somewhere safe, take advice and make sure you only take as large a risk as you are comfortable with.

Earning more

If your life plan is at all ambitious, it will probably involve doing more not less. Whilst many suggestions and ideas here won't cost you anything, you probably do want to earn more. Moonlighting in some sectors is almost the norm. However, this can jeopardise your relationship with your employer. It can also leave you very little time to enjoy yourself, as moonlighting literally means burning the midnight oil!

You need then to consider ways in which you can earn more. Some listed below are painfully obvious but equally, embarrassingly easy to overlook. Others are more challenging but all are possible.

10 ways to increase your income without moonlighting

1. **Ask for a rise** – Oh so obvious but ask yourself, when did you last negotiate a pay rise?

2. **Change jobs** – Sometimes you have to move to a new employer to be really valued. This is because once you've been anywhere a while, you can often get taken for granted.

3. **Gain a qualification** – It's been proven that people who demonstrate their development by gaining a qualification end up better paid. Join a professional institute or consider a part-time university course.

4. **Move towns** – If your employer operates from many sites, consider transferring to a new location. Joining a new team can bring all the benefits of changing jobs with fewer of the risks.

5. **Seek extra responsibility** – Making your current job bigger will enable you to ask for more money. Remember, you might need to prove you can handle the extra responsibility before looking for reward.

6. **Link pay to performance** – Share some of your boss's risk by linking your pay to your performance. Are you brave enough to do this?

7. **Rent out the spare room** – Clear out the junk and get yourself a lodger. It's the only way many young people

can afford to leave home. Check out the tax benefits of renting out a room in your home.

8.   **Make your home a film set** – You don't have to live in a castle or moated manor to make money from your home as a film set. Location agencies need ordinary settings as well as the unusual.

9.   **Generate electricity** – This is going to become increasingly important. Solar, wind and geothermal are all ways you can generate your own power. You can sell what you don't use back to the power companies.

10. **Spend less** – If nothing else on this page appeals, you might have to turn back to discover how you can reduce your expenditure.

Debt

The chances are that you're starting your life plan from a position you're not totally happy with. For most of us, debt is one of those things we want less of. Debt and the worries it may generate can dominate your life. Getting out from under the black cloud of debt is for many a key life plan objective.

Here are some tips to help you do just that.

10 ways to get out of debt

1. **Cut spending** – You need to free up cash to repay those loans. Look for economies in your monthly budget.

2. **Reduce interest** – Many debt consolidation loans are at a high interest rate and simply put all of your rotten eggs in one rotten basket. Your best option is to increase your mortgage and pay off the expensive loans. Never do this without taking proper advice.

3. **Renegotiate** – Taking you to court is not an easy option for your creditors. See if you can renegotiate the deal. Most big companies have teams who help those unable to pay.

4. **Make a budget** – It often helps illustrate your problem if you write down your monthly income and outgoings and show this to major creditors. If they know you why you can't pay, they're more likely to be sympathetic.

5. **Check it's yours** – Unless you've signed a loan agreement, or incurred the expense yourself, you might not be liable for the debt. Married people, for example, are not automatically liable for each other's debts.

6. **Plead ignorance** – If you were deliberately misled and that can be proved in court, you might not have to pay the debt. Take legal advice.

7. **Garnishee order** – If you're in debt because a business owes you, it's possible to apply in court for a garnishee order against one of their customers. This means the customer pays you, not the business it owes.

8. **Keep talking** – Ignoring debt just makes people angry. Keep in touch with your creditors and tell them honestly how things are.

9. **Resist pressure** – The law is very strict when it comes to chasing debts. Do not give in to bullying by one creditor; it can make matters worse.

10. **Take advice** – There are lots of advice agencies able to help you cope with debt. Some can negotiate with creditors on your behalf.

Serious debt

If you are facing lots of debts, there are some creditors that need to be paid ahead of the others. The people who shout the loudest or send the most demanding letters are not always the ones you should treat as a priority. There are some people you do need to put at the top of the pile. They include your landlord or mortgage lender, so that you do not lose your home, basic services such as electricity and phone, and your car if you rely on it to get to work. In general, the first debts to deal with are those that, if unpaid, would push you into a worse situation than you are in right now.

If you're considering responding to one of the many TV ads that offer debt consolidation services, remember that these companies often charge hefty fees. These are rolled into the consolidated debt so you can afford them. Some people also consider bankruptcy, always take professional advice before committing yourself.

And finally

Money is in reality nothing more than a means of exchange. Its value lies in what it enables you to do. On its own it can do little to enhance your life plan. Setting goals that reduce your debt, increase your spare cash and perhaps even save for the future might all form part of your life plan. Remember though that your greatest life plan achievements will probably not be to have a pile of money in the bank!

Home

Your home is the place where you probably plan to feel the most relaxed. It's where you go to be alone, as well as where you choose to entertain friends. Your life plan will inevitably involve taking a fresh look at your home, as well as the things you might do there. If you share your home, it also needs to be an amalgam of both of your respective plans and ideals. It can also be good if you share you home and have sufficient room, for each person to have their own personal space as well. We all need to be alone sometimes.

You might have lived in your current home for decades, or alternatively have only recently moved in. You might live in a house, flat, boat, mobile home or single room. Whatever kind of home you have, you will want it to be comfortable, to feel like it's yours, and to have within it the things you treasure most. One of the challenges is how to achieve this without spending lots of money or being distracted from your other objectives.

Being comfortable

Comfort means different things to different people. There are things that make most people feel comfortable, yet often we're too busy to think about them. Here are some small things you can introduce to your life at home that might make you feel more comfortable. If they feel more like special treats to you, that's OK. It simply means you can use them to reward yourself when you reach a particular milestone.

10 small things that make life more comfortable

1. **Get up late** – Have a lie-in at least once a week. Consider varying your working hours to break the routine. Changing from your usual routines can make you feel more in control of your life and not governed by the clock.

2. **Fluffy towels** – Chuck out those threadbare towels and step out of the shower each morning into a large fluffy towel. Start the day feeling really good.

3. **Shop online** – Save time, fuel and the hassle of the big weekly supermarket shop and order your groceries online. Even with a delivery charge it works out cheaper than driving to the shop. Spend the time you save doing something more enjoyable.

4. **Fresh orange juice** – Squeeze an orange and make breakfast special on at least one day each week. Alternatively brew fresh coffee. The preparation of both can be enjoyed almost as much as the product.

5. **Nice music** – We rarely need encouragement to buy CDs or MP3 downloads, but why not listen to music more often and set the scene for the day? Alternatively, if you always have the radio or TV on, try a day without and see how different it feels.

6. **Valet the car** – For less than the cost of a tankful of fuel, you can have your car valeted inside and out. It's almost as nice as having a new car.

7. **Grow herbs** – A sunny windowsill is all you need. They enable you to enliven the meals you cook and even those you microwave straight from the freezer! Fresh herbs are easy to grow and add a Mediterranean touch to your cooking.

8. **Write letters** – Shun email and text occasionally. Buy some nice paper and a pen and write letters to a friend. Keep the replies to read again.

9. **Soak in the bath** – Add something scented, light some candles, turn off the phone and soak for an hour. If there's room, soak with your partner.

10. **Have early nights** – Retire early with a good book or simply go to sleep and dream. Leave those household chores until tomorrow.

Making it yours

Our homes often evolve as our interests and lifestyle change. A home with young children, for example, is very different from that same home 20 years later when they've left and their parents are on their own again.

Whatever stage of life you are at, you might choose to take a fresh look at your home. Ask yourself if it actually feels like home, or just the place you sleep and spend some time. If someone who didn't know you walked in, what would they conclude about you? Compare this with what you would *like* that stranger to conclude. Most importantly of all, ask yourself what would make it feel more like your home. Here are some ideas to consider.

10 small ways to make your home really feel like home

1. **Photos on the wall** – Hang some of your favourite photos on the wall. They could be of family, friends or occasions you've enjoyed. Having them on display will remind you of happy times.

2. **Plant things** – Gardens can become a chore, but even small changes to the garden you might have inherited will make it feel like yours. Unless gardening is your passion, choose things that are easy to maintain.

3. **Welcome on the doormat and a light in the porch** – This will make your visitors feel more welcome. It will also act as your beacon, guiding you those last few metres home.

4. **Choose the colour** – You might not like the colour scheme you've inherited. Don't change it all at once though, simply choose some colours you like and start with the areas that bother you most.

5. **Think about furniture** – Few can afford to buy lots of new furniture, yet over time, what you have wears and becomes out of date. Don't be afraid to buy the odd item rather than trying to do it all at once. It doesn't take much to make a difference. Make a start with a few colourful cushions or rugs.

6. **Chuck stuff out** – Those family cast-offs we all furnish our first homes with have a habit of lingering for years. Sometimes it can be as good to lose stuff as to buy it!

7. **Books everywhere** – If you have lots of books, put them on display. Buy books on subjects you are passionate about and be surrounded by your interests and fascinations.

8. **The big screen** – If you love movies, why not make your home your cinema? Have friends round, buy popcorn and you'll always have the best seats.

9. **Candles, incense sticks, wind chimes** – It's good to be in touch with your inner self. As well as lighting candles to calm yourself, use them as scene setters when you entertain. Create a relaxing environment

10. **Travel trophies** – If you've travelled the world, or would like to, why not put the evidence on your wall? Remember your travels every time you walk into the room.

Making your home special

Like it or not, we all look at each other's homes and make subjective judgements as a result. If our home looks special, it not only satisfies our natural urge to impress, but it also makes us feel good as well. Having made your home your own, you might choose to make it special by adding those all-important finishing touches.

Making your home special doesn't have to involve spending lots of money. In fact some things suggested here will cost you next to nothing. Special doesn't have to mean expensive.

10 affordable ways to make your home feel special

1. **Garden lights** – These can be solar powered, so environmentally friendly. Lights around the garden make your home seem special and mean you can enjoy favourite plants after dark.

2. **Bolder paintwork** – Make sure there are no planning restrictions first, but a more assertive colour scheme will suit your more confident lifestyle. Make your front door stand out from others in your street.

3. **Low voltage lights** – Use low voltage lighting and lamps to create areas of light and shadow around your home. Many have built-in transformers so can simply replace existing fittings. Others can be plugged into the wall.

4. **Cushions** – Large cushions scattered around your living room will make it easy to flop on the floor and get really comfortable. Great for romantic evenings!

5. **Mirrors** – Strategically placed mirrors (opposite windows) will make each room feel larger and lighter. This is a bonus if you have a small flat, or simply want the place to feel lighter.

6. **Classic colours** – When decorating your home, choose colours that you know you can live with. Bold colours can look great in the tin but shock you when on the

wall. (Unless you buy a sample pot to test first.) Think about your home, your style, your taste and if in doubt, err on the side of caution. What's important is that you choose the colours, rather than live with what's already there.

7. **Less is more** – It's always better to have a few very nice things than a house full of bric-a-brac. Be brutal and chuck some stuff out.

8. **Old is good** – Why not see if your parents or other older relatives have some nice things they'd let you have for your home. Alternatively, visit some junk shops in search of a bargain. The way old things wear over time creates a nice contrast with what is bright and new.

9. **Awards** – Without being boastful, it's good to display framed awards or photographs of you meeting someone famous. They create talking points as well as reminding you of special occasions.

10. **Flowers** – Why not make sure you always have some fresh flowers? You might put them on the table, or even beside your bed. Don't go overboard with big arrangements, just a few single stems in a vase will create the same effect.

Clutter

Surrounding yourself with much loved objects makes your home feel yours and also, perhaps rather special. There is a danger though, that if you continue to add new things, without clearing out some of the old, your home will become increasingly cluttered.

Removing clutter from your home, and indeed your life, can be intensely satisfying. It can also be quite traumatic as you linger over some things you've hung on to for a long time.

If your life plan involves taking on new challenges, it might also be good to include de-cluttering as well. Not quite a fresh start, but a positive step in the direction you've decided to go.

10 ways to de-clutter your home

1. **Start somewhere easy** – Empty all your kitchen cupboards. Replace everything that's still in date that you think you'll use. Chuck the rest. There's little emotional attachment to groceries!

2. **Go car booting** – Collect stuff from around your home you know you won't use and turn it into cash. Do not buy anything when you're there.

3. **Read and recycle** – Magazines and other reading material (apart that is from books) should be read then recycled. Tear out any interesting pages.

4. **Hire a skip** – Once you've committed to a skip it seems a waste not to fill it to the brim. Go through your home, garage and garden and fill the skip. Consider sharing a skip with neighbours and making it an annual event.

5. **Don't be too sentimental** – If aging relatives give you things that mean a lot to them, they're only trying to help. However, you want your home to reflect your own happy memories not theirs. Tactfully take what is offered, but don't feel duty bound to put it all on display.

6. **Clean your PC** – Don't forget to de-clutter your PC. Delete programs you don't use and archive to CD files not in regular use. Free disk space.

7. **Accept your mistakes** – Everybody buys clothes they never wear. Don't keep these shopping skeletons in your closet. Take them to a charity shop or sell them on Ebay™.

8. **Clear the shelves** – Have you seen those small china ornaments that people used to buy at the seaside years ago? Each is different and bears the crest of the resort where it was bought. Have you built up a collection of souvenirs and gifts you've been given but would rather lose? Why not put them away as part of your new look.

9. **Give stuff away** – We all buy gadgets with every intention of using them regularly. Reality is often different though. Have you got things you know deep down you'll never use? Why not give them away to a charity shop?

10. **Have a bonfire** – If you have a large garden, a bonfire is a fun way to really enjoy seeing your clutter disappear.

Keeping tidy

Tidiness is considered a virtue by many and a challenge by the rest of us. It's certainly good to follow a good de-clutter with a concerted effort to avoid replacing the stuff you've just got rid of.

The biggest benefit of tidiness is that you can usually find things more easily. Here are some tips to help you keep things tidy.

10 top tidiness tips

1. **Bin household bills** – Once you've paid a bill, shred or burn it. The same applies to payslips, personal bank statements and greetings cards.

2. **Be logical** – Put new groceries at the back, not the front of the cupboard. That way, you can't hoard old packs.

3. **Buy cupboards** – Have storage space for what you want to keep. When it's full, throw something out before putting anything new in its place.

4. **Don't use paper** – Filing things on your PC rather than printing them out saves paper. Digital files and photographs are usually easier to find as well.

5. **Say no** – People are constantly offering you things: gifts, product samples and memorabilia. Practise politely saying no.

6. **Keep contracts** – Don't lose any current legal agreements. You might one day want to prove what has been agreed. Put them somewhere safe.

7. **Tax records** – Unless you use an accountant, you need to retain papers that relate to your tax. They're useful when you need to query something about your pay and deductions.

8. **Guarantees** – You often need a copy of both the invoice and guarantee before warranty work can be

carried out or faulty appliances replaced. Create a file and when the warranty period runs out, throw the paperwork away.

9. **Remember the car** – It's no good sorting out your home and leaving your car in a mess. Clear out the mess and take rubbish with you when you park and pop it in a bin. Don't let it collect between the seats.

10. **People** – Your personal network is a huge asset. Consider using software to keep your address book and key dates in order. Make it easy to remember things about the people who matter most to you.

Your home then, can become much more than your castle. You've made it more comfortable, made it feel like home, added some special things and without spending a fortune transformed it (or at least made a start!).

These days, we tend to move home every few years, so clutter doesn't accumulate in the way it did in the past. However, a tidy home is also a home where you can find the things you want and need, without being distracted by the stuff you'd rather forget.

Hopefully as you improve your home, it will become better able to re-energise you. You will then be better equipped to work on the other aspects of your life plan.

Retirement

When you pass 60, or perhaps 55, you enter what is now widely termed the 'third age'. This is because during a lifetime you spend:

- 20 years growing up and learning
- 40 years earning
- 20 or more years in the 'third age'

Of course, lives these days do not fall into distinct separate segments like this any more. In fact, as you're planning to change your life, you may not want to retire in the conventional sense. This chapter is more about the opportunities open to you when you reach the 'third age'. If you're younger, they can form part of your long-term planning. If you're there already, then you have the opportunity to do them now.

Planning for the future

However old you are, it's never too soon or too late to plan for later. When the time comes to take life a little easier and perhaps focus more on fun than work, you want to be in as strong a position as possible.

Here are some things to think about and how you might deal with each one.

10 tips when planning your own future

1. **You're old a long time** – It's not unusual to live to 90 and a good few make it beyond 100. Recognise that you will probably be 'old' for a long, long time.

2. **Beat inflation** – Previous generations have had life savings all but wiped out by the effects of inflation. Discuss with your advisers how to inflation-proof your old age. Don't just expect your company pension to provide for all your needs.

3. **Keep saving** – Enjoy today, but also try to build a nest egg for when you no longer want to work. Saving is easiest if done little and often. Make saving a habit.

4. **Protect your home** – You may not want to be paying a mortgage or rent when you're retired. Ask yourself how you might plan to have no big debts when you're ready to retire.

5. **Good friends** – Friendships become more important as you grow older. Recognising that it's sometimes harder to make new friends when you're very old might encourage you to work harder at the relationships you want to keep.

6. **Keep fit** – It's amazing how the human body functions so well for so long. Get fit and stay fit, however old you are now. Investing in your fitness now will pay dividends later.

7. **A bungalow by the sea** – Have you wondered why people retire to the coast? Ask yourself now if you'll

want to move away when you stop working. It might be worth moving sooner. Weigh up the options.

8. **Think of the kids** – If you have a family, how will they figure in your future plans? Consider discussing it with them now, in case they see things differently.

9. **You might live alone** – If you live with a partner, one usually dies first. Discuss what you might do and agree together how you'll deal with it when it happens.

10. **Make a will** – However little you have, making a will encourages you to discuss your wishes with a lawyer. Wills also save time and hassle for your family at a particularly stressful time.

Volunteering

If you choose to retire, you suddenly find yourself with time on your hands. This can feel very strange and even unsettling after a long and busy life. One way you can fill your time and develop new interests is to volunteer.

Volunteering is not just about helping other people. It's also about helping yourself. Volunteering gives you new experiences, enables you to learn new things and introduces you to new people.

There are many volunteering opportunities around, so you need to be sure to choose the ones that are best for you. It's also wise to pace yourself and not overcommit yourself. This is easy to do in the initial months when you're possibly missing the routine of work.

To help you plan ahead, or make good use of the time you can spare now, here are some tips on volunteering.

10 volunteering opportunities that will help you

1. **First aid** – It's noble to learn how to save lives. It's fun to get to an event free because you're one of the first aid team. There are several organisations that recruit, then train and place volunteer first-aiders. Check them out.

2. **Art** – If you've an interest in art, music or old buildings, volunteer to be an usher at your local theatre or a room guide in a stately home. You can enjoy your favourite art as often as you'd like, all for free!

3. **School** – There are countless opportunities to help young people. From hearing them read to mentoring undergraduates. Contact your local education centres and offer to help. You'll learn more than you teach!

4. **Families** – Befriending a family with particular needs (perhaps they are asylum seekers) gives you an insight into other lives. In return you can help them interpret the world they now find themselves living in.

5. **Prison** – Volunteer to visit offenders who otherwise would see no one from the outside world. Take an interest in them and understand how they might struggle to improve their lives.

6. **Charities** – Find a charity that does work you feel is important and offer your help. You might do practical work, help with fundraising or even become a Trustee.

7. **School governor** – Like charity Trustees, school governors are effectively the school's non-executive board. In a small school, you'll be quite hands-on. In a larger one, you'll probably be involved with just one or two facets of school life.

8. **Sport** – Only a small number of sports organisations can afford staff; most rely on the goodwill of willing volunteers. Some need extra people for special events. For example, with training you could be a race marshal and enjoy a trackside view of your favourite motorsport.

9. **Hospitals** – Visit people in hospital who have no family and are lonely. You will speed their recovery and be reminded that life for you is perhaps not too bad. Most hospitals have a befriending service to make the introductions.

10. **Advocacy** – Work with disadvantaged people to make sure their views are heard and their needs fully met. Advocates work with all kinds of people. It broadens your perspective on the place where you live.

Winding down

At some point in your life, you will decide to wind down. You will likely be looking for less stress, less responsibility and more freedom. You probably won't be looking for an abrupt change to your life. That's what used to happen when people were working full-time one day and retired completely the next.

Here are some tips to consider now, so that when the time comes, you can make a smooth transition into eventual retirement.

10 ways to make a smooth transition

1. **Work fewer hours** – The obvious way to edge towards retirement is to take more time off, but keep working. This taper into retirement can suit employers as well as employees. Organise it well ahead though, otherwise your employer might make other plans.

2. **Realise a dream** – If you work in an office but have always wanted to drive a bus, now's your chance. Retire from the office and drive that bus. In fact many traditionally low-paid service jobs really suit the otherwise retired. Try something really different.

3. **You can do, so teach** – Passing on your knowledge and experience to younger people is very rewarding. You can teach in school, university, prison and many other places. You can do this for pay or as a volunteer; it depends on your needs and your interests.

4. **Marry people** – If you follow a particular faith, it might be possible to become a minister. If faith plays an important part in your life, look at ways to get more involved in your faith group as you spend less time at work.

5. **Emigrate** – Moving to a cheaper, warmer country can make retirement possible when otherwise it would be impossible. Why not teach English when you get settled? It would be a great way to get to know people.

6. **Write** – Not everyone can write books, but everyone has a story to share. Alternatively, write articles for magazines that cover your specialist interests.

7. **Volunteer** – You might not need the money, just the mental stimulation. There are thousands of volunteering opportunities. Some are listed in this chapter.

8. **Start a business** – If the job you want isn't out there, create it yourself. Start a business that gives you the lifestyle and income you need. If you have a pension, you won't need or want to work full-time. This flexibility gives you much more scope.

9. **Non executive directorships** – Many public bodies pay non execs to spend around 50 days per year contributing to their strategic focus. Why not build yourself a portfolio of part-time appointments?

10. **Travel** – Either as a tourist or maybe a tour guide. Guides travel for free!

Goal setting when you're older

You never stop having ambitions and goals. They just change as you grow older. In fact, we all make plans for the future, but sometimes we wait too long before actually doing them. Setting goals for the future is important, but so too is avoiding the temptation to put things off. It would be disappointing if when the time came, you no longer had the stamina!

It's also fair to say that as we get older we become more cautious and risk averse. Here are some things you might not have tried yet that you might consider adding to your 'don't wait too long' list of ambitions.

10 things to do before it's too late

1. **Kiss and make up** – Family feuds can run long and deep. Ideally, they need to be resolved before it's too late. Be brave and make the first move.

2. **Have an exotic holiday** – Has there always been a reason for putting off that safari or scuba diving trip? Now you have to make the time, find the money and go. Bring back lots of mementoes.

3. **Overcome a phobia** – If you've always been afraid of something, get help and confront it head on. You'll find this amazingly liberating.

4. **Eat à la carte** – If you always avoid those expensive restaurants, make sure you visit one at least once. Dress up and make it an occasion. Don't worry about the bill.

5. **Gamble** – If you've never put money on a horse, why not do it just once. Are there other things you've never tried that it wouldn't hurt to do just once? Don't risk you health, wealth or relationship, but if you're normally very timid, be bold at least once.

6. **Your family tree** – It'll fascinate you and keep future generations informed about those who came before them.

7. **Fly in a small plane** – If you've only flown in airliners, you'll be amazed at how different a two-seater feels.

Hire a small plane and fly over your home. Take lots of photographs.

8. **Give unconditionally and anonymously** – Giving money to a good cause without recognition or thanks is the purest form of giving you can do. Practise first with small donations that you do get thanked for.

9. **Forgive your parents** – This one's deep; it's also tough. Many of us go through life blaming our parents for our shortcomings. Forgive them.

10. **Write your story** – Those around you will think they know you pretty well, but you know yourself best. Why not write your life story down? Make it as simple or as complex as you like. Use the excuse to reflect, remember and record. You don't have to share it, just tuck it away.

Making it happen

Creating and following your life plan is no small feat. When you start to set long-term life goals, they can seem so far away as to be completely out of reach. This can make the very process quite daunting. Don't panic though, the answer is to take things one step at a time.

Everybody's life plan will be different. We all start from somewhere different, because no two lives are identical. Equally, as ambitions and goals also vary widely, each individual's plan will contain quite different steps. That's why this book contains literally hundreds of simple steps you can take to make life a little better. You simply put them in whatever order you want to deliver the change you're seeking.

Most will start at the beginning, defining success and perhaps more importantly, freeing up some valuable planning time. You will also find that the length of step you take will depend on the aspect of your life under scrutiny. Some aspects of self development seem easier than others. Remember though that what you find easy, others may find more challenging and vice versa. This is a very individual project.

For many people, work will be the main bugbear. Here though, the checklists present you with a number of options: make things better where you are; go somewhere different; or start doing your own thing. As you go through your life, you might choose to revisit this and other chapters of the book. Life after all is a progression, and the lists and topics that meet your needs today will be different from those you will find most useful in a few years' time. The sections regarding relationships, children and parents are key examples of this.

As you use this book, why not personalise it with your own notes, comments and dates in the margins? Use sticky notes to mark pages and add your comments if you need more room. You can then look back in the years to come and revisit some of your hopes, fears, ambitions and challenges. Remember that a life plan is for life, not just the next six months. Good luck!